# Credit & General
# ENGLISH

The Scottish Certificate of Education Examination Papers
are reprinted by special permission of
**THE SCOTTISH QUALIFICATIONS AUTHORITY**

ISBN 0 7169 9297 3
© *Robert Gibson & Sons, Glasgow, Ltd., 1999*

**ROBERT GIBSON · Publisher**
17 Fitzroy Place, Glasgow, G3 7SF.

SCOTTISH
CERTIFICATE OF
EDUCATION
1994

MONDAY, 9 MAY
1.00 PM – 1.50 PM

# ENGLISH
# STANDARD GRADE
General Level
Reading
Text

Read carefully the passage. It will help if you read it twice. When you have done so, you should answer the questions. Use the spaces provided in the Question/Answer booklet.

# CONTENTS

*In this extract, the writer describes his return to Spain during the Spanish Civil War, the welcome he receives there and the surprising outcome.*

1    In December 1937 I crossed the Pyrenees from France—two days on foot through the snow. I don't know why I chose December; it was just one of a number of idiocies I committed at the time. But on the second night, near the frontier, I was guided over the last peak by a shepherd and directed down a path to a small mountain farmhouse.

2    It was dark when I reached it—a boulder among boulders—and I knocked on the door, which was presently opened by a young man with a rifle. He held up a lantern to my face and studied me closely, and I saw that he was wearing the armband of the Republican side.

3    "I've come to join you," I said.

4    The young man slung his rifle over his shoulder and motioned me to enter the hut. A dark passage led to a smoky room. Inside, in a group, stood an old man and woman, another youth with a gun, and a gaunt little girl about eleven years old. They were huddled together like a family photograph fixing me with glassy teeth-set smiles.

5    There was a motionless silence while they took me in—seeing a young tattered stranger, coatless, soaked to the knees and carrying a kit-bag from which a violin bow protruded. Suddenly the old woman said "Ay!" and beckoned me to the fire, which was piled high with glowing pine cones. I crouched, thawing out by the choking fumes, sensing deeply this moment of arrival.

6    "Will you eat?" asked the woman.

7    "Don't be mad," said her husband.

8    He cleared part of the table, and the old woman gave me a spoon and a plate. At the other end the little girl was cleaning a gun, frowning, tongue out, as though doing her homework. An old black cooking-pot hung over the smouldering pine cones, from which the woman ladled me out some soup. It was hot, though thin, a watery mystery that might have been the tenth boiling of the bones of a hare. As I ate, my clothes steaming, shivering and warming up, the boys knelt by the doorway, hugging their rifles and watching me. Everybody watched me except for the gun-cleaning girl who was intent on more urgent matters. But I could not, from my appearance, offer much of a threat.

9    Gradually, a light joky whispering seemed to fill the room. "What are you?"

10    "I'm English."

11    "Ah, yes—he's English."

12    They nodded to each other with grave politeness.

13    "And how did you come here?"

14    "I came over the mountain."

15    "Yes, he walked over the mountain ... on foot."

16    They were all round me at the table now as I ate my soup, all pulling at their eyes and winking, nodding delightedly and repeating everything I said, as though humouring a child just learning to speak.

17    "He's come to join us," said one of the youths; and that set them off again, and even the girl lifted her gaunt head and simpered. But I was pleased too, pleased that I managed to get here so easily after two days' wandering among peaks and blizzards. I was here now with friends.

18    The people in the kitchen were a people stripped for war—the men smoking beech leaves, the soup reduced to near water; around us hand-grenades hanging on the walls like strings of onions, muskets and cartridge-belts piled in the corner, and open orange-boxes packed with silver bullets like fish. War was still so local then, it was like stepping into another room. And this was what I had come to re-visit. But I was now awash with sleep, hearing the blurred murmuring of voices and feeling the rocks of Spain under my feet. The men's eyes grew narrower, watching the unexpected stranger, and his lumpy belongings drying by the fire.

19      Then the old woman came and took me by the elbow and led me upstairs and one of the boys followed close behind. I was shown into a small windowless room of bare white-washed stone containing a large iron bed smothered with goatskins. I lay down exhausted, and the old woman put an oil lamp on the floor, placed a cold hand on my brow, and left me with a gruff good-night. The room had no door, just an opening in the wall, and the boy stretched himself languidly across the threshold. He lay on his side, his chin resting on the stock of his gun, watching me with large black unblinking eyes. As I slipped into sleep I remembered I had left all my baggage downstairs; but it didn't seem to matter now.

20      I was awoken early next morning by the two armed brothers who were dressed for outdoors in ponchos of rabbit skin. They gave me a bucket of snow to wash in, then led me gingerly downstairs and sat me on a stool where the old lady poured me some coffee. The little girl, her hair brushed and shining already, was fitting ammunition into cartridge-belts. As I drank my coffee—which tasted of rusty buttons—she looked at me with radiant slyness.

21      "He came over the mountains," she said perkily, nodding to herself. The boys giggled, and the old man coughed. They brought me my baggage and helped me sling it over my shoulders, and told me that a horse and cart were waiting for me outside.

22      Then the boys half-marched me into the lane and the rest of the family followed and stood watching, blowing on their purple fingers. The old woman and child had bright shawls on their heads, while, for some reason, the old man wore a tall top hat. The boys helped me into the back of the cart and climbed up after me. The driver sniffed, and uncoiled his whip.

23      "Horse and cart," said one of the brothers, nudging me smartly. "We've got to save your legs. They must be half destroyed with all this walking over mountains. And what have we got if we haven't got your legs? You wouldn't be much use to us, would you?"

24      I was beginning to get a bit bored with all this levity, and sat there silent and shivering. The boys perched close beside me, one on each side, holding their guns at the ready, like sentries. Every so often they pointed them at me and nodded brightly. They appeared to be in a state of nervous high spirits. "Vamanos!" snarled the driver, and shook up the reins crossly. The old man and his wife raised their hands solemnly and told me to go with God. The little girl threw a stone at the horse, or it may have been at me, but it hit the horse and caused it to start with a jerk. So we began to lumber and creak down the steep rocky lane, the brothers now holding me by either elbow. The Pyrenees stood high behind us, white and hard, their peaks colouring to the rising sun. The boys nodded towards them, grinning, nudging me sharply again, and baring their chestnut-tinted teeth.

25      Through the iced winter morning, slipping over glassy rocks, we made our stumbling way down the valley, passing snow-covered villages, empty and bare, from which all life and sound seemed withdrawn. This chilling silence was surely not one of nature, which could be broken by a goat-bell or the chirp of a bird. It was as if paralysing pestilence had visited the place, and I was to notice it on a number of occasions in the weeks to come. It was simply the stupefying numbness of war.

26      After an hour or so we came to a small hill town still shuttered by the shadow of rocks. A bent woman crept by, bearing a great load of firewood. A cat shot through a hole in a wall. I noticed that the brothers had suddenly grown tense and anxious, sitting straight as pillars, thin-lipped, beside me. Two militiamen, in khaki ponchos, came out of a doorway and marched ahead of us down the street. Even our driver perked up and began to look around him with what appeared to be an air of importance. The militiamen led us into the square, to the dilapidated Town Hall, from which the Republican flag was hanging. The brothers called out to a couple of sentries who were sitting on the steps, and one of them got up and went inside. Now for a proper welcome, I thought. I got down from the cart, and the brothers followed. Then four soldiers came out with fixed bayonets.

27      "We've brought you the spy," said the brothers, and pushed me forward. The soldiers closed round me and handcuffed my wrists.

Adapted from *A Moment of War* by Laurie Lee

*[END OF PASSAGE]*

## QUESTIONS

### Write your answers in the spaces provided.

**Look at Paragraph 1.**

1.  What difficulties did the writer face on his journey into Spain?

    (i) *it was December*

    (ii) *and snowing*

**2 1 0**

**Look at Paragraph 2.**

2.  **Write down two** pieces of information which suggest that there was a war on.

    (i) *a man opened the door with a rifle*

    (ii) *an armband of the Republicans*

**2 1 0**

**Look at Paragraph 4.**

3.  Explain, **in your own words**, **two** ways in which the people seemed as if they were arranged for a "family photograph".

    (i) *all alongside each other*

    (ii) *gathered closely.*

**2 1 0**

**Look at Paragraphs 5 to 8.**

4.  Explain, **in your own words**, the effect in Paragraph 5 of the writer's appearance and possessions on the family.

    *The family appear to be poor and don't seem to possess many possessions.*

**2 1 0**

5.  The gun-cleaning girl was "intent on more urgent matters" (Paragraph 8).
    **Write down two** words or expressions which show how intent she was.

    (i) *frowning*

    (ii) *as though doing her homework*

**2 1 0**

*Marks*

6. The writer felt that his appearance couldn't "offer much of a threat" (Paragraph 8). Give **two** reasons why he should feel this way.

    (i) on his own.

    (ii) he was cold and wet and had little possessions.

| 2 | 1 | 0 |

**Look at Paragraphs 9 to 16.**

7. At first, the family **seemed** to treat the writer seriously. What evidence is there that they **did not really believe** what he said?
Give **three** examples.

    (i) repeating everyting he said

    (ii) winking

    (iii) nodding

| 2 | 1 | 0 |

**Look at Paragraph 18.**

8. The people were "stripped for war".
**In your own words**, give **two** pieces of information which support this statement.

    (i) grenades hanging from the walls

    (ii) cartrige-belts piled in the corners

| 2 | 1 | 0 |

9. (a) Why is the expression "silver bullets like fish" a particularly suitable one for the writer to use in this situation?

    Sardines

| 2 | 1 | 0 |

(b) **Write down** another expression from the same paragraph which conveys a similar idea.

| 2 | ■ | 0 |

*Marks*

**Look at Paragraph 19.**

**10.** Why do you think the writer felt "it didn't seem to matter now" that he had left his baggage downstairs?

he was so tired now and the others were scared of him.

2 | 1 | 0

**Look at Paragraphs 20 and 21.**

**11.** Explain as fully as you can how the little girl's attitude towards the writer had changed from the previous day.

She was now far more sarcastic than she was before

2 | 1 | 0

**Look at Paragraphs 22 to 24.**

**12.** "I was beginning to get a bit bored with all this levity" (Paragraph 24).

Explain **in your own words** what the writer means by this.

All their sarcasm and jokes towards him making him look little

2 | 1 | 0

**13.** The brothers and the old couple treated the writer in a different way. **Explain the difference** as fully as you can. (You should refer to speech and behaviour.)

(*a*) The brothers stayed close to him with their rifles at the ready, full of sarcasm

2 | 1 | 0

(*b*) The old couple were also full of sarcasm. They didn't really have time for him

2 | 1 | 0

Marks

**14.** "The boys perched close beside me" (Paragraph 24).

The writer might have used "sat" rather than "perched". Explain why "perched" is a better word here.

*ready to pounce, or shoot.*

2 1 0

**Look at Paragraph 25.**

**15.** What were the **two** effects on the villages of the "stupefying numbness of war"?

2 1 0

(i) *empty and bare*

(ii) *chilling silence*

**Look at Paragraph 26.**

**16. In your own words**, suggest one reason why the brothers had now grown "tense and anxious".

*As they were getting nervous as they came closer to the militamen*

2 ■ 0

**17. Write down** an expression which shows that the writer did not expect to be handed over as a spy.

*'Now for a proper welcome'*

2 ■ 0

**Think about the whole passage.**

**18.** Explain clearly how the events of this story are likely to add to the writer's feeling that he had committed "a number of idiocies" (Paragraph 1).

*He came in winter when it was snowing and cold. He turned up at any old house.*

2 1 0

*[END OF QUESTION PAPER]*

SCOTTISH
CERTIFICATE OF
EDUCATION
1995

WEDNESDAY, 3 MAY
1.00 PM – 1.50 PM

ENGLISH
STANDARD GRADE
General Level
Reading
Text

Read carefully the passage.  It will help if you read it twice.  When you have done so, answer the questions.
Use the spaces provided in the Question/Answer booklet.

*Timothy, Jane, and their mother, Rose, have found an old cottage with a sign:  "FOR RENT OR SALE.  APPLY TO BEACH HOUSE, WALLNEY."  The children have persuaded Rose—against her better judgement—to enquire about renting it, even though it has stood empty for years.*

1    Quarter of a mile up the path, they came to the village of Wallney.  Not much of a village: four big farmhouses, a couple of rows of flint-and-brick cottages, pub, sub-post office and an old-fashioned red phone-box.  But enough to half-restore Rose's sanity.  The owner of the cottage wouldn't want to let it just for a week, or even a fortnight.  This was no holiday cottage.  The thought brought relief.

2    But there stood Beach House, one of the four farmhouses.  Well kept, but not a working farm.  Weeds grew in front of the barn doors.  Rose walked up the tidy front garden, and knocked on the door of the little glass porch.  Too late, she realised the front door was never used.  The porch was full of potted plants, several big ones right in front of the door itself.

3    An inner door opened, and a grey-haired woman in spectacles appeared.  Respectable-dowdy, with sharp blue eyes and a very stubborn mouth.  She gestured angrily, indicating some other entrance that should be used.  It put poor Rose one-down from the start.  She blundered for a long time round the barns and farmyard, trying to find a way through, until finally the woman opened a door in a six-foot wall, and looked at her as if she was an idiot.

4    "We've come," faltered Rose, "about renting the cottage.  Only for a week or a fortnight . . ."  She was almost ready to take to her heels and run.  Only the small eager figures on each side of her kept her steady.

5    "Oh, come in," said the woman impatiently, and led the way with vigorous but erratic steps, as if she had arthritis but was trying to trample it underfoot by sheer will-power.

6    The kitchen they were led into was uncannily like the one they had just seen in the old cottage, except it was shining and alive.  There was a glowing coal fire, which cheered Rose up, even in the middle of July.  A grandfather clock ticked soothingly.  There was a bundle of knitting in a chair, and a tray laid for tea, with a glass sugar-basin.  Various chairs were occupied by various teddy-bears, one wearing full-size spectacles.

7    And straightaway, Rose was under a spell.  This indeed was her granny's kitchen come again.  She felt very small, but very safe.

8    "Sit down, sit down," said the woman irritably.

9    They sat, careful not to inconvenience the teddy-bears.

10    "We're interested in the cottage, Mrs . . ."

11    "Miss," said the woman decisively, as if that disposed of marriage for good and all.  "Miss Yaxley.  Were you thinking of renting or buying?  Renting is thirty pounds a week;  buying is fifteen thousand including the furniture thrown in."

12    Rose gasped at such bluntness.

13    "What's it called?"

14    "Beach Cottage. Belonged to my brother. Just inherited it under his will. *I've* got no use for it. Takes me all my time to keep this place going, at my time of life. Much too much for me. Much too much."

15    "We thought we'd like to try it for a week . . ." said Rose. "To see if the children like it. Then perhaps . . ."

16    She was sure this woman would sweep away her nonsense with a flood of biting common sense. But Miss Yaxley seemed to be very much in two minds. She turned aside, and rubbed at a tiny spot on the chrome teapot, as if it was annoying her intensely.

17    "It's no place for children," she said in a low voice. "My brother was an old man . . ."

18    "I think it's great," said Timothy, turning on his most charming smile like a searchlight. He had a swift eye for adult indecision. But Rose thought for once Timothy had overreached himself. Miss Yaxley gave him a grim look, as if to say children should be seen but not heard. She seemed to come to a decision and Rose was sure the answer would be no.

19    So she was all the more amazed when Miss Yaxley said, "Very well. I don't suppose a week can do any harm." She was still vigorously rubbing away at the spot on the teapot, which showed no sign of moving. Then she said, rather grudgingly but also rather guiltily, "I'll only charge twenty pounds for the first week. You'll have to clean the place up. Men live in *such* a muddle. They're *hopeless*. But I'd like the rent in advance. Weekly in advance."

20    There was more thissing and thatting, but in the end Miss Yaxley drove them back herself in her battered Morris Minor with the dry bird-droppings turning into rust-stains on the bonnet. Rose thought that, having made her mind up, Miss Yaxley was not only keen to get them into the cottage, but also curiously keen to get rid of them.

21    They were done and settled in by nine. The children had truly amazed her. Rose was astonished that children could work so hard. Still, the whole thing *had* been their idea.

22    Timothy, who was practical like his Dad, had discovered a drum of paraffin in a lean-to, filled the oil-lamps and got them going. He used more paraffin, in a careful calculating way that brought her out in a cold sweat, to get the fire in the kitchen range going. He had also got the water-pump over the sink to work. At first it had only made disgusting wheezing sounds, but Tim had poured water down it from a butt in the garden, calling it "priming the pump" very professionally. At first it had pumped evil rusty red stuff, but now it ran clear, though Rose had visions of outbreaks of cholera and typhoid, and hurried dashes to the hospital in Norwich, and how would you ever get an ambulance up that path, but if you boiled all the water . . . Now he was winding up all the clocks and really getting them ticking.

23    And Jane had sweated up the path many times with the luggage and then gone with a huge list of groceries to the sub-post office, and staggered back again, still without complaint, and even thought to buy all available hot-water bottles. And boiled huge black kettles, and shoved all the hotties into the beds, which did seem quite clean, thank God, only awfully dusty and sneeze-making. Now she used the black kettle again to make tea, and settled down to drink hers.

24    "We're a nine-days' wonder in the village," she announced. "Everybody staring at me and yak, yak, yak behind their hands. The woman in the shop asked me how long we were staying, and when I said only a week to start with she said, 'Just as well, my girl, just as well.' What on earth do you think she meant by that?"

Adapted from *Yaxley's Cat* by Robert Westall

[*END OF PASSAGE*]

## QUESTIONS

**Write your answers in the spaces provided.**

**Look at Paragraph 1.**

1. **Write down two** pieces of information which show that Wallney was "not much of a village".

    (i) _empty, hardly anything in the town_

    (ii) _the owner wouldn't let for less than 2 weeks_

    Marks: 2 1 0

2. How can you tell from this paragraph that Rose did **not** want to rent the cottage?

    _It says 'the thought was a relief'_

    Marks: 2 1 0

**Look at Paragraph 2.**

3. **Write down two** pieces of information which show that Beach House was "well kept, but not a working farm".

    (i) Well kept _Rose walked up the "tidy front garden"_

    (ii) Not working _the front door was never used_

    Marks: 2 1 0

4. Explain fully how Rose could tell that "the front door was never used".

    _plants were positioned outside the front door_

    Marks: 2 1 0

**Look at Paragraphs 3 to 5.**

5. Miss Yaxley seemed unfriendly. **Write down two** expressions which show this.

    (i) _gestured angrily_

    (ii) _she looked at Rose as if she was an idiot_

    Marks: 2 1 0

6. Describe, **in your own words, two** ways in which Rose was affected by Miss Yaxley's behaviour.

    _was made nervous and a bit scared. And forgot what she was going to say._

    Marks: 2 1 0

*Marks*

**Look at Paragraphs 6 to 12.**

**7.** The kitchen was "alive". How does the writer develop this idea in the rest of Paragraph 6?

"glowing coal fire", "grandfather clock ticked soothingly"

| 2 | 1 | 0 |

**8.** Explain fully why Rose felt "very small, but very safe". (Paragraph 7)

She was still a bit nervous with the woman but the kitchen reminded her of her granny's which made her feel at home.

| 2 | 1 | 0 |

**Look at Paragraph 15.**

**9.** (*a*) From the way Rose spoke, what can you tell about her feelings?

didn't know how long he want

| 2 | ■ | 0 |

(*b*) How does the writer show this?

"Then perhaps

| 2 | 1 | 0 |

**Look at Paragraphs 16 to 18.**

**10.** (*a*) Explain, **in your own words,** how Rose expected Miss Yaxley to react to her enquiry.

That she would say no. And tell her to leave

| 2 | 1 | 0 |

(*b*) How in fact did Miss Yaxley react? Explain as fully as you can.

Miss Yaxley had two different thoughts of it, She wasn't sure

| 2 | 1 | 0 |

**11.** Describe **two** ways in which Timothy tried to persuade Miss Yaxley to let them rent the cottage.

| 2 | 1 | 0 |

(i) *"I think it's great!"*

(ii) *"turning on his most charming smile"*

**12.** What made Rose think that Timothy had "overreached himself"? Explain **in your own words**.

*that Timothy had tried something that wouldn't work*

| 2 | 1 | 0 |

**Look at Paragraph 19.**

**13.** "I'll only charge twenty pounds for the first week." Why did Miss Yaxley say this

(*a*) "rather grudgingly"? *she was charging a bit much*

| 2 | ■ | 0 |

(*b*) "rather guiltily"? *then realised what she'd done.*

| 2 | ■ | 0 |

**Look at Paragraph 22.**

**14.** Give **three** pieces of evidence which show that Timothy was "practical like his Dad".

| 2 | 1 | 0 |

(i) *discovered the paraffin and used it in a calculating way.*

(ii) *He got the water pump in the sink to work*

(iii) *getting the clocks to work.*

**15. Write down one** expression which shows that Timothy knew what he was doing.

*very professionally*

| 2 | ■ | 0 |

13

*Marks*

**16.** Look at the sentence beginning "At first it had pumped evil rusty red stuff . . .".

Show how the writer creates an impression of uneasy thoughts rushing through Rose's mind

(*a*) by word choice. _evil, rusty , stuff_

2 1 0

(*b*) by sentence structure.

2 1 0

**Look at Paragraph 23.**

**17. Write down one** word or expression which shows that Jane worked hard.

"Staggered back again, still without complaint"

2 ■ 0

**18.** Why do you think the writer has used the word "and" so often in the first two sentences of this paragraph?

to emfisise *(emphasise)* the amount of joss that she was doing

2 1 0

**Think about the whole passage.**

**19.** Think carefully of all you learn about Miss Yaxley.

Tick (√) **one** word from the list below which **you** think describes her best, and give a reason for your choice.

| excitable | | friendly | | unusual | √ |

| greedy | | patient | |

she didn't have time for anyone and had old fashioned views about children being seen and not heard, she liked to make people feel small.

2 1 0

14

*Marks*

**20.** The woman in the shop told Jane it was "just as well" they were staying at the cottage for only a week to start with. (Paragraph 24)

**From your reading of the whole passage**, explain as fully as you can what **you** think she meant by that.

As it wasn't much of a house and Miss Yaxley would be on your back every minute of the day.

| 2 | 1 | 0 |

*[END OF QUESTION PAPER]*

SCOTTISH CERTIFICATE OF EDUCATION 1996

TUESDAY, 7 MAY
1.00 PM – 1.50 PM

ENGLISH
STANDARD GRADE
General Level
Reading
Text

Read carefully the passage. It will help if you read it twice. When you have done so, answer the questions. Use the spaces provided in the Question/Answer booklet.

*The following article has been adapted from "The Scotsman" newspaper, June 1994.*

# Washed away

**There was a time when almost every Scottish seaside resort had an outdoor swimming-pool, but now there are only a few and their long-term future is threatened. BRIAN PENDREIGH reports**

1   TWO seagulls hang in the blue sky overhead. For a moment or two they are motionless beneath the white wisps of cloud. One turns its head and screams something to its mate, some seagull joke about the sanity of those humans in the water perhaps.

2   It is 3pm on Saturday and at this precise moment there are three people in the open-air swimming pool at North Berwick, tiny figures bobbing about in the vast blue expanse of water. There are many more shivering beneath towels around the perimeter. The pool was one of the town's most important tourist attractions. They had galas here, swimming and diving displays that pulled in big crowds.

3   It still has its regulars. Two old women turn up with raincoats over their swimming costumes, so they can get into the pool as quickly as possible. Two old men do synchronised swimming. Others bring the staff sweets or baking. But numbers have been falling for years. Costs are high and the season is short. East Lothian District Council is subsidising the swimmers to the tune of almost £10 a time.

4   Now the council has decided to build a modern indoor pool and close one of Scotland's last remaining open-air pools. It has been there since 1900, an essential part of the North Berwick landscape for generations of holiday-makers.

5   There was a time when almost every seaside resort had an outdoor pool, overflowing with noisy, splashing bodies in the summer months. They were part of Scotland. They are part of our social history. But the bodies have disappeared into leisure pools and onto charter flights to Majorca, and the open-air pools have disappeared in their wake.

6   Anstruther, Arbroath, Buckhaven, Macduff, Prestwick, Saltcoats; they all had their own pools. There must have been dozens of them once. There were separate men's and women's pools at St Andrews, but mixed bathing was widely accepted by the time most pools were built in the Thirties when interest in healthy outdoor activities took off.

7   Portobello Pool opened in 1936 and was considered one of the wonders of the age. It had a diving platform 33 ft above the water, four chutes, four springboards and band music was relayed from Princes Street Gardens. The wave machine was so powerful it soaked the poolside dignitaries on the opening day.

8   The pool became a national attraction and there were 18,000 admissions on a single day, just 4,000 fewer than the number of admissions for the whole of the pool's final summer in 1978. Particularly in the early days, many went merely to spectate or sunbathe, though, unlike some pools, Portobello was heated from the outset, using steam from the adjoining power station. Sean Connery worked as a lifeguard for a while. Now both pool and power station have gone.

Cool customers: there is a breeze sweeping across the pool and the teenagers are shivering violently. But then that is because they are speaking to a journalist and not in the warmed water.

9    North Berwick pool will probably open in 1995 for the last time. Other outdoor pools survive at Stonehaven and Gourock, but neither's long-term future is secure.

10    Stonehaven had 86,000 admissions in 1934, its first year, though three-quarters were spectators. Initially the water was unheated, untreated seawater, changed every few days "as it became dirty". The following year it was filtered, disinfected and heated, and the number of people actually going into the pool almost doubled.

11    In 1990, there were 25,000 admissions. In 1993 there were 14,000. The decline would be worse if it were not for the successful reintroduction of special midnight swimming sessions, which had been abandoned in the Seventies because of drunkenness.

12    At North Berwick attendances have fallen steadily over the past five summers, from 21,177 swimmers in 1989 to 8,154 in 1993. "It will be a great sin if this pool closes. This is character-building stuff in here," says Pat Macaulay, who has swum regularly in the pool since childhood and is here with her new season-ticket and her children Richard and Joanna. Pat Macaulay spent the summers of her youth in and by the pool. It was *the* meeting place, *the* social centre for the young people of the town.

13    There is a drop or two of rain in the air and a breeze sweeping across the exposed location beside the harbour. Is it not rather cold? "The water is fine," says Macaulay. "A lot of it is mind over matter . . . I think the kids are getting a bit soft these days."

14    But there are few adults in evidence at this session. The vast majority are children and teenagers, who form lines by the chute and springboard at the deep end.

15    They complain that the new leisure pools do not have these features, the new pools are smaller and the Royal Commonwealth Pool too far away. They are shivering violently. "That's because we're out here speaking to you," says one. "When you're in it's brilliant." Journalistic integrity demands his claim be put to the test.

16    It is not the cold that hits you, but the mouthful of salt water, as you disappear beneath the surface for the first time. The pool is heated, though not as warm as some indoor pools. But some indoor pools are too warm for strenuous swimming. North Berwick is fine as long as you keep moving. There is something quite pleasant in swimming along on your back listening to the chat of the gulls. It is cold when you get out. The knack is to get dried immediately afterwards and not hang around talking to journalists.

17    Shona MacDonald, the pondmaster, and her assistant Michelle Smith have an enormous affection for North Berwick. "The people love it here," Smith says. "We would buy it ourselves if we had the money."

18    However, East Lothian's director of leisure and tourism, says: "Outdoor pools are very expensive to run and declining in terms of attractiveness."

19    The council is building an indoor pool at Musselburgh and is not reopening the outdoor pool at nearby Port Seton. Work has begun on a £2 million pool beside North Berwick's sports centre with opening scheduled for 1996. It will be open all the year round and is expected to have at least 75,000 admissions annually.

20    The director accepts there is some regret in the town at the decision to close the open-air pool, but adds that there have been no formal protests. "People are just being rather nostalgic. The pool has had its day. It's part of a former era."

21    Within the next few years the area occupied by the open-air pool may be returned to its natural state of rocks and sea. The gulls will have a different landscape to discuss. Only rocks and sea remain forever, but the old landscape will undoubtedly linger in the memory of all those whose guts filled with seawater on a chilly Scottish summer's day.

*[END OF PASSAGE]*

*Marks*

## QUESTIONS

### Write your answers in the spaces provided.

**Look at Paragraphs 1 to 4.**

1. According to the writer, what might the seagulls think of the people in the water?

   _____     2 ■ 0

2. In Paragraph 2, the writer tells us that there are only three people in the water. Why do you think he also mentions the exact time, and the day?

   _____     2 ■ 0

3. **Write down** an expression which emphasises the size of the open-air pool at North Berwick.

   _____     2 ■ 0

4. How can you tell that there are no longer galas at the pool?

   _____     2 ■ 0

5. Give **two** reasons why East Lothian District Council decided to close the open-air pool.     2 1 0

   (i) _____

   (ii) _____

6. The open-air pool has been "an essential part of the North Berwick landscape for generations of holiday-makers".

   **Write down** an expression from earlier in this section which conveys the same idea.

   _____

   _____     2 ■ 0

**Look at Paragraphs 5 and 6.**

7. "There was a time when almost every seaside resort had an outdoor pool . . ."

   Explain how the writer continues this idea in paragraph 6.

   _____

   _____     2 1 0

*Marks*

8.  **In your own words**, explain the reasons given for the disappearance of open-air pools.

    _____

    _____

    _____    2 | 1 | 0

**Look at Paragraphs 7 and 8.**

9.  **Write down three** pieces of information which show why Portobello Pool was considered "one of the wonders of the age".    2 | 1 | 0

    (i) _____

    (ii) _____

    (iii) _____

10. **Write down** an expression which shows that Portobello Pool was popular with people from all over the country.

    _____    2 | ■ | 0

**Look at Paragraphs 10 and 11.**

11. **In your own words**, give **two** reasons why the number of swimmers at Stonehaven Pool increased in 1935.    2 | 1 | 0

    (i) _____

    (ii) _____

12. What was the effect of the "reintroduction of special midnight swimming sessions"?

    _____

    _____    2 | 1 | 0

**Look at Paragraphs 12 and 13.**

13. How do the attendance **figures** given in paragraph 12 show that the writer is closely interested in North Berwick Pool?

    _____    2 | ■ | 0

*Marks*

**14.** Pat Macaulay says, "This is character-building stuff in here".
**Write down** something else she says which continues this idea.

_____

2 ∎ 0

**15.** "It was *the* meeting place, *the* social centre . . ." (Paragraph 12)
The writer uses italics to show that the word "*the*" has a particular meaning here. What do you think that meaning is?

_____

2 ∎ 0

**Look at Paragraphs 14 to 16.**

**16.** What things do young people dislike about the new leisure pools?

_____

_____

2 1 0

**17.** "When you're in it's brilliant." (Paragraph 15)
(*a*) How does the writer test this claim?

_____

2 ∎ 0

(*b*) Explain why he feels the need to test it.

_____

_____

2 1 0

**18.** (*a*) **Write down two** things the writer seems to like about North Berwick Pool.

2 1 0

(i) _____

(ii) _____

(*b*) **Write down two** things he seems to dislike about it.

2 1 0

(i) _____

(ii) _____

*Marks*

**Look at Paragraph 20.**

**19.** " . . . there is some regret . . . at the decision to close the open-air pool"

    (*a*) **Write down** another expression from this paragraph which indicates people's feelings about the closure.

_____

2 ■ 0

    (*b*) Explain **in your own words** what this expression tells you about people's feelings.

_____

_____

2 1 0

**Think about the passage as a whole.**

**20.** This article was taken from a newspaper.

    **Write down** any **three** features of it which are typical of a newspaper article.

2 1 0

    (i) _____

    (ii) _____

    (iii) _____

**21.** Explain how the title relates to the content of the passage.

_____

_____

_____

2 1 0

**22.** (*a*) What unusual idea does the writer use at the beginning and ending of the passage?

_____

_____

2 1 0

    (*b*) What effect does this have?

_____

_____

2 ■ 0

*[END OF QUESTION PAPER]*

SCOTTISH
CERTIFICATE OF
EDUCATION
1997

WEDNESDAY, 7 MAY
1.00 PM – 1.50 PM

ENGLISH
STANDARD GRADE
General Level
Reading
Text

Read carefully the passage.  It will help if you read it twice.  When you have done so, answer the questions.
Use the spaces provided in the Question/Answer booklet.

## Tunes For Bears To Dance To

1    Henry had been impatient for the cast to be removed so that he could return to his job as the bender for Mr Hairston at the Corner Market.  Mr Hairston had a back problem and found it hard to bend over.  Henry did the bending for him.  Picked up whatever fell on the floor.  Reached for merchandise on the lower shelves to fill the customers' orders.  He also had other duties.  Helped unload the boxes and crates that arrived from the wholesalers.  Stocked the shelves.  Bagged the potatoes in the cellar, then carried them upstairs to the produce section.  Mr Hairston was proud of his produce.  Fresh lettuce and carrots and spinach and such extras as parsnips and mushrooms, all of them in neat display at the rear of the store.

2    Henry worked at the store every day after school and on Saturday mornings.  Until, that is, he had broken his kneecap, tripping, then falling down the bottom steps of the house just as school ended in June.  A hair-line fracture, the doctor had said, nothing serious, but serious enough for a cast that enclosed his calf and knee.  Mr Hairston said he would keep his job open until his knee was healed.

3    "How will you bend over?" Henry had asked.

4    "I won't stock the lower shelves until you come back."

5    "Who'll sweep the floors and put up the potatoes?"

6    Mr Hairston had scowled without answering.  He scowled most of the time, his expression as sour as the pickles in the wooden barrel near the cash register.

7    Five weeks later when Henry reported to the store without his crutches, ready for work, Mr Hairston merely grunted.

8    "Potatoes to bag up," he called over the shoulder of a customer, and Henry made his way down to the cellar, where a bin of potatoes awaited him.  He always tried to hurry the job because the cellar was dark and damp and he often heard rats scurrying across the floor.  One day, a grey rat squirted out of a bag of potatoes and Henry had leapt with fright, his heart exploding in his chest.  He was afraid of a lot of things — the closet door that never stayed closed in his bedroom, spooky movies about vampires — but most of all, the rats.

9    When he came back upstairs, Mr Hairston was saying goodbye to a customer Henry recognized as Mrs Pierce, who lived on the first floor of his tenement.  Smiling and nodding, Mr Hairston led her to the door and closed it softly after her.

10    "Disgusting, the wart on her chin, hairs growing out of it," he said, returning to the register, a sneer replacing the smile.  Actually, his smile was merely a rearrangement of his lips, his usual sneer turned inside out.  Henry was amazed at how Mr Hairston treated his customers.

11    "The customer's always right," he proclaimed one day, as if he could read Henry's mind.  "But only in the store.  When buying.  Otherwise, they're only people.  Stupid, most of them.  Don't even know a bargain when they see one.  So, why give them a bargain?"

12    He handed Henry a candy bar, which astounded the boy because Mr Hairston had never before given him a treat. "Eat," he said. Then, "It was nice with the customers during the war, though. Rationing. People came running if they heard I had got butter in. Or cigarettes."

13    Henry listened, his cheeks bulging with the candy while Mr Hairston looked off, as if he were talking to himself, his voice almost dreamy. "I'd make them line up. Make them wait, acting like the stuff hadn't arrived yet but was expected any minute. All the time the order was here and they waited in line. I was like a dictator, the way they treated me. I *was* a dictator. Because I had control over them." Then looking down as if discovering Henry's presence after having forgotten him there, he said, "Go to work. I don't pay you to hang around doing nothing."

14    Just before closing time, while Henry was sweeping the floor, Mr Hairston's daughter came into the store. She appeared at the back door, having descended from the tenement above, where Mr Hairston lived with his wife, whom Henry had never seen, and the girl, whose name was Doris. Doris was a whisper of a girl, slender, with long black curls that reached her shoulders, a bow in her hair. It always looked like the same bow but the colours were different, red and yellow and blue, bright and vivid colours in contrast with her pale, white face, the dark eyes deep in their sockets, like the windows of a haunted house.

15    She usually came and went like a ghost, appearing suddenly and then fading away, a door closing softly behind her or the rustle of her clothing faint in the air. Sometimes he didn't see her at all but sensed her presence somewhere in the store. She was a year ahead of him in school and when they met in the corridor she lowered her eyes and looked away. She always carried library books in her arms. In the store he sometimes felt those haunted eyes upon him, turned and almost saw her, then heard the back door closing softly. They had never spoken a word to each other.

16    Whenever Mr Hairston saw her in the store, he would order her to leave. "Upstairs," he'd command, his hand pointing to the ceiling.

17    That afternoon the girl spoke to Henry for the first time, a brief word, "Hello." So brief and whispered that at first he doubted his ears. She didn't smile at him but her expression changed, or rather an expression of some kind filled the usual blankness of her face. He could not read that expression. As she turned away before he could return her greeting — if it *had* been a greeting — he noticed a bruise on her cheek, purple and ugly.

18    "What happened to your cheek?" he asked, whispering for some reason.

19    "Upstairs!"

20    Mr Hairston's voice was like thunder in the quiet store and Henry leapt with surprise as he turned to confront the store owner, whose face was dark with anger.

21    Henry began to sweep furiously and heard the girl's footsteps fading, the door opening and closing.

22    "She fell down," Mr Hairston said while Henry swept the same spot over and over. "Clumsy girl, always hurting herself."

23    A late customer entered the store and Mr Hairston turned away, cursing beneath his breath. He hated last-minute customers.

24    That night Henry thought of Doris, who was clumsy and fell down a lot and hurt herself. He prayed to keep her safe from harm.

Adapted from *Tunes For Bears To Dance To* by Robert Cormier

*[END OF PASSAGE]*

**Marks**

## QUESTIONS

### Write your answers in the spaces provided.

**Look at Paragraphs 1 and 2.**

1. Why had Henry been "impatient"?

    *because he wanted his cast off.*

    2 1 0

2. Why did Mr Hairston need a "bender"?

    *Mr Hairston had a back problem.*

    2 1 0

3. (a) **Write down three** things Henry did as part of his "other duties".

    2 1 0

    (i) *Unload boxes + crates*

    (ii) *Stock shelves*

    (iii) *Bagged potatoes.*

    (b) How does the writer's sentence construction in Paragraph 1 draw attention to the variety of actions Henry has to carry out?

    *Short, sharp, sentaces*

    2 1 0

**Look at Paragraphs 7 and 8.**

4. **In your own words** describe how Mr Hairston first greeted Henry on his return to work.

    *He didn't really show any expression.*

    2 1 0

5. What **three** things did Henry dislike about the cellar?

    2 1 0

    (i) *it was dark + damp*

    (ii) *heard rats*

    (iii) _____

25

Marks

6. "... a grey rat squirted out of a bag of potatoes ..." (Paragraph 8)

(a) What is unusual about the writer's use of the word "squirted" in this sentence?

_it seems as if the rat is a liquid_    2 ■ 0

(b) Why is it a particularly suitable word to use here?

_It shows the rats sly, evil, squirmy_    2 ■ 0

**Look at Paragraphs 9 to 11.**

7. (a) Describe Mr Hairston's **behaviour** and **attitude** towards Mrs Pierce while she was in his shop.    2 1 0

(i) Behaviour _kind, Caring,_

(ii) Attitude _~~nicely~~_
_kind, Caring,_

(b) Explain fully how these changed once she had left.    2 1 0

(i) Behaviour _two-faced, rude_

(ii) Attitude _disgusting, selfish, rude_

8. **Write down** the **one** word the writer uses which most clearly shows that Mr Hairston's smile was not genuine.

| Harrangement |    2 ■ 0

9. (a) What is unusual about the writer's sentence construction in Paragraph 11?

_short sentences, brisk words_    2 ■ 0

(b) What does the writer's use of this construction suggest about Mr Hairston's character?

_abrupt._    2 ■ 0

26

**Look at Paragraphs 12 and 13.**

10. (a) What was Mr Hairston's **real** reason for thinking "it was nice with the customers during the war"?

   *He was in control, people needed him.*

   | 2 | 1 | 0 |

(b) Give an example of his behaviour which supports your answer to (a).

   *" I was a dictator "*

   | 2 | ■ | 0 |

11. While talking about wartime, Mr Hairston "looked off . . . his voice almost dreamy".

   What else did he do which suggests he had been day-dreaming?

   *Forgotten henry was there.*

   | 2 | ■ | 0 |

**Look at Paragraphs 14 and 15.**

12. (a) Doris is described as a "whisper" of a girl.

   What do you think the writer means by this?

   *She is quiet, like a ghost*

   | 2 | ■ | 0 |

(b) In Paragraph 14, what comparison does the writer use to describe her eyes?

   *windows of a haunted house*

   | 2 | ■ | 0 |

(c) **Write down three** other words or expressions from Paragraph 15 which the writer uses to convey a similar idea about Doris.

   (i) *appearing suddenly*

   (ii) *fading away*

   (iii) *Sensed her presence*

   | 2 | 1 | 0 |

13. **Write down** the **two separate words** which best convey the contrast between Doris's face and her bows.

   | ~~bright~~ bright | and | dark |

   | 2 | ■ | 0 |

14. Give **two** pieces of evidence which suggest that Doris was shy.

   (i) *They had never spoke*

   (ii) *lowered her eyes, looked away*

   | 2 | 1 | 0 |

**Look at Paragraphs 17 and 18.**

15. (a) What unusual thing happened that afternoon?

_The girl spoke to him_

2 | 1 | 0

(b) Explain **in your own words** why Henry "doubted his ears".

_because he'd never talked to her before_

2 | 1 | 0

(c) **Write down** an expression from later in Paragraph 17 which repeats this idea of doubt.

_brief_

2 | ■ | 0

16. When Henry asked Doris about her cheek, he whispered "for some reason".
What reason do you think he had for whispering?

_She was shy._

2 | ■ | 0

**Look at Paragraphs 20 to 24.**

17. Mr Hairston's face was "dark with anger".
What other expression is used in this paragraph to show his anger?

_voice was like thunder_

2 | ■ | 0

18. "Henry began to sweep furiously" (Paragraph 21)
". . . Henry swept the same spot over and over" (Paragraph 22)
What do Henry's actions tell you about how he felt?

_He felt sorry for Doris, And angry at Mr Hairston._

2 | 1 | 0

19. "'She fell down,' Mr Hairston said . . ." (Paragraph 22)
**From your reading of the whole passage**, do you believe Mr Hairston? Give a reason for your answer.

_I don't believe him, as he seems a very nasty character. And even when henry asked a question about her cheek he shouted at Doris to get upstairs._

2 | 1 | 0

[*END OF QUESTION PAPER*]

SCOTTISH
CERTIFICATE OF
EDUCATION
1998

WEDNESDAY, 6 MAY
1.00 PM – 1.50 PM

# ENGLISH
# STANDARD GRADE
General Level
Reading
Text

Read carefully the passage overleaf.  It will help if you read it twice.  When you have done so, answer the questions.  Use the spaces provided in the Question/Answer booklet.

# Why You Don't See Baby Pigeons

1    When I moved to a flat in New York and discovered that my new neighbours included a colony of pigeons, my first reaction was:  exterminate the brutes!  I cringed at their morning mating calls, and agreed with my wife, Dana, when she cursed them as winged rodents that soil the city.  I attacked them with broom and water-pistol.  It was hard for me to believe that the traditional symbol of peace, a dove with an olive branch, is actually a white pigeon.

2    Then last December, after scaring away a grey pigeon roosting on the sill of our bathroom window, I found a nest there with an egg in it.  "Revenge is ours!"  I shouted to Dana, triumphantly holding the egg aloft.  "Should I smash it right away or save it for an omelette?"

3    But Dana was looking in horror at the window-sill behind me.  The pigeon had swooped back to the empty nest and was beating its wings against the window frame.

4    "You put that back this second!" Dana said, with the same look on her face that I swear the parent pigeon had.

5    "How can a rational human want to save a baby pigeon?" I asked as I returned the egg.

6    And then it came to me.  Here was a chance to answer the perennial mystery that puzzled generations of city dwellers:  why doesn't anyone ever see a baby pigeon?  Let others plumb Loch Ness for its monster or climb the Himalayas in search of the Yeti.  I would be the first human to see a baby pigeon in the wild.

7    The bird roosted outside the bathroom for a week, and then one morning the nest was empty—no mother, no baby, no egg.  Soon another nest appeared with two eggs, but they, too, vanished.

8    I began keeping a field journal, and named the grey pigeon Medea and her black-and-white speckled partner Don Guano.  On March 12 Don Guano strutted about, following Medea in circles around the living-room ledge.  Finally he mounted her for a second or two, flapping his wings—for balance, I suppose, unless he was just happy.

9    Two days later an egg appeared, followed shortly by a second.  Don Guano and Medea settled into a domestic routine.  From late morning until late afternoon he sat on the eggs while she went off.  The rest of the time, she roosted while he brought twigs for home-improvement projects.

10    Then, after ten days of roosting, Don Guano and Medea abruptly abandoned the nest.  The next day the eggs were gone without a trace.

11    I reported the parenting troubles to Margaret Barker of the Cornell Laboratory of Ornithology.  "Eggs normally hatch after 18 days," she said, "but sometimes pigeons are frightened off the nest, and sometimes eggs never hatch because the parents aren't getting the proper diet to make sturdy eggshells."

12    "And why," I asked, "do we never see a baby pigeon?"  "They stay in the nest for the first month," Margaret told me, "and grow so rapidly they're nearly full size when they emerge."

13    When Medea returned, I fed her a bowl of cereal mixed with a powdered calcium supplement.  I worried about what this was doing to me.  Was I becoming one of those people on park benches who feed pigeons?

14     Soon the calcium-enriched Medea laid two more eggs, and this time the roosting proceeded smoothly for the full 18 days. We were ready to make history on Friday, April 21. I armed myself with a new pair of binoculars and a copy of *The Pigeon* by Wendell Mitchell Levi, which I studied with all the care other parents devote to Dr Spock's books.

15     "Wherever civilisation has flourished, there the pigeon has thrived," wrote Levi. Pigeons are found on every continent except Antarctica, inhabiting environments from Alaska to the equatorial islands. They were worshipped in Mesopotamia and sculpted on Egyptian tombs. They carried messages for King Solomon, helped Julius Caesar conquer Gaul and won dozens of medals for combat service during the Second World War.

16     Pigeons, or "rock doves", can fly up to 75 miles per hour and find their way home from more than 1000 miles away. Their primary reference seems to be the position of the sun, which correlates with a pigeon's biological clock. But they can navigate even under overcast skies by sensing the earth's magnetic field. There are "reverse commuter" pigeons, urban pigeons that fly 30 miles a day to fields and grain silos outside the city, then return to roost in town.

17     They are social animals, living in colonies because they gain protection from predators. Poets have praised pigeons' lifelong devotion to their mates. Tennyson linked their iridescent feathers with romance and rebirth in his famous couplet:

> *In the spring a livelier iris changes on the burnish'd dove;*
> *In the spring a young man's fancy lightly turns to thoughts of love.*

18     I quoted those lines to Don Guano and Medea as we waited on that crucial Friday in April. But by evening, neither egg had hatched. I feared the worst. Next day at noon, however, as I watched Don Guano settle in for his shift on the nest, I spotted a bit of golden fuzz moving underneath him.

19     It was a shaggy little creature, lying in a heap along with the eggshell it had just escaped. "Miracle of miracles!" I wrote in my journal. "Yes, New York, there is a baby pigeon." I had never been an animal lover and was not particularly fond of naturalists or the endangered species they were trying to save. So why pigeons?

20     The answer did not occur to me until I visited New York's most glamorous bird, the peregrine falcon, 57 floors above the streets. There was no doubting this bird's power, particularly after seeing the ***pigeon*** feathers in the nest—the remnants of victims captured in mid-air and fed to the falcon chick. But as I looked at the falcons, all I could think was: *You wimps! You wouldn't be here without us! We've spent millions on you; we've banned the DDT that was upsetting your delicate systems; we've built you nest boxes; we've coddled your chicks—all to produce two dozen birds in New York. One pigeon colony achieved that in my courtyard by itself.*

21     A lot of people in the city may identify with the falcon: a ruthless, grandly isolated predator, rewarded with a penthouse view of its dominion. But the falcon doesn't hold the great secret to evolutionary success, at least not for humans.

22     Our species did not prevail over other animals by being brave and cunning solitary hunters. We used our brains to become co-operative and shameless opportunists, able to adapt to any available niche. We may pollute and squabble and crowd together in grimy crannies without views, but at least we're survivors. We may envy their speed and rapacity, but we are not falcons. We are tougher. We, fortunately, are pigeons.

Adapted from a New York Times article by John Tierney

[END OF PASSAGE]

## QUESTIONS

### Write your answers in the spaces provided.

**Look at Paragraphs 1 to 5.**

1.  (a) **Write down** an expression from **Paragraph 1** that clearly indicates **the writer's attitude** to pigeons.

    _He wanted to 'exterminate the brutes'. This shows how strongly the writer felt._

    2 ■ 0

    (b) Given his attitude, what **fact** about pigeons did the writer find difficult to understand?

    _that the sign of peace is a white pigeon._

    2 ■ 0

2.  (a) "Should I smash it right away or save it for an omelette?" (Paragraph 2)
    What was Dana's reaction to these suggestions?

    _mortified, ordered him to put it back right away_

    2 ■ 0

    (b) Why is her reaction surprising? _We are told she had 'cursed them as winged rodents', suggests she felt as strongly 'anti-pigeon' as her husband_

    2 1 0

**Look at Paragraph 6.**

3.  Why does the writer begin **Paragraph 6** with such a short sentence?

    _Because he just realised something and this shows a change of view._

    2 ■ 0

4.  What expression used later in the same paragraph means almost the same as "perennial mystery"?

    _puzzled generations_

    2 ■ 0

*Compares birth of a baby pigeon to the sightings of LN monster or Yeti (2 well known mythical creatures)*

Marks

5. Explain how the writer tries to make the rest of **Paragraph 6** funny.

By adding that others would have to go far to look for lochness, monster The Yeti etc, while he would be the first human in in the world to see a baby pigeon on his doorstep.

2 1 0

**Look at Paragraphs 7 to 10.**

6. What evidence is there that the writer started to take a closer interest in the pigeons?

2 1 0

(i) He watched /examined the nest 4 weeks

(ii) kept a field journal

(iii) He named them + followed their moves on the nest.

7. "he brought twigs for home-improvement projects" (Paragraph 9)

(a) Explain exactly what Don Guano was doing.

bringing twigs ~~for~~ to build the nest

2 1 0

(b) To what is (Don Guano) being compared, and what is the effect of this comparison? *man doing DIY*

To a human, the husband/wife roles that they showed.

2 1 0

*It adds humour*

**Look at Paragraphs 11 to 14.**

8. (a) Why might pigeon eggs **not** hatch after 18 days?

2 1 0

*Put in own words!*

(i) pigeons are frightened off the nest.

(ii) not right diet to make sturdy eggshells

(b) Why don't we normally see a baby pigeon?

They stay in the nest for the 1st month and grow so rapidly they're nearly full size when they emerge

2 1 0

33

*Marks*

9. What, do you think, was **the writer's attitude** to "those people on park benches who feed pigeons" and how does he reveal it?

his attitude was shocked and didn't want to be those people who had nothing else to do but feed pigeons

2 1 0

10. (a) **Write down two** things the writer did to ensure that the eggs hatched successfully.

2 1 0

(i) he fed Medea cereal + calcium supplement,

(ii) ~~took them to~~ Margaret Baker asked advice from

(b) What kind of books do you think Dr Spock wrote?

Childcare

2 1 0

**Look at Paragraphs 15 to 18.**

11. "Wherever civilization has flourished, there the pigeon has thrived" (Paragraph 15) What fact proves this statement?

Pigeons are in every continent apart from Antartica

2 1 0

12. What **two** things help pigeons to navigate?

2 1 0

(i) position of the sun

(ii) sensing the earths magnetic field

13. Explain why "reverse commuter" is a good way of describing urban pigeons.

2 1 0

Marks

**14.** Explain **in your own words** why poets have praised pigeons.

*Poets praised pigeons dedication forever to their mates*

2 | 1 | 0

**Look at Paragraphs 19 to 22.**

**15.** (*a*) Why does the writer call peregrine falcons "wimps"?

*because he thinks they havnt doneanything by themselves*

2 | 1 | 0

(*b*) What **two** things about the way **Paragraph 20** is written show the strength of his feelings?

2 | 1 | 0

(i) *his short remarks*

(ii) *re-using the word "we've"*

**16.** (*a*) **In your own words**, explain why a lot of people might "identify with the falcon".

*They might because the falcon is a tough character, with but lots of faults*

2 | 1 | 0

(*b*) Explain, as clearly as you can, why the writer believes that most human beings are more like pigeons than falcons.

*because we work hard like pigeons to achieve something!*

2 | 1 | 0

35

*Marks*

**Think about the passage as a whole.**

17. Complete the following sentences to show the changes in the writer's attitude towards pigeons.

    (i) To begin with the writer ___hated them___.

    (ii) Later he ___tried to understand them___.

    (iii) Finally he ___realised he could relate to them___.

    `2  1  0`

18. Tick (✓) **one** of the following words and explain why **you** think it is the best one to describe this passage. Give evidence from the passage to support your answer.

    informative ☐     surprising ☐     thought-provoking ✓

    ___At the end he mentions that___
    ___we are just like pigeons___

    `2  1  0`

[*END OF QUESTION PAPER*]

SCOTTISH
CERTIFICATE OF
EDUCATION
1999

FRIDAY, 30 APRIL
1.00 PM – 1.50 PM

# ENGLISH
## STANDARD GRADE
General Level
Reading
Text

## AN IMPORTANT MESSAGE FROM
## THE SCOTTISH QUALIFICATIONS AUTHORITY

**"Following concerns expressed by schools and individuals regarding the content of the 1999 General Level English paper, it has been decided not to publish it."**

SCOTTISH
CERTIFICATE OF
EDUCATION
1994

MONDAY, 9 MAY
2.30 PM – 3.20 PM

ENGLISH
STANDARD GRADE
Credit Level
Reading
Text

Read carefully the passage. It will help if you read it twice. When you have done so, answer the questions. Use the spaces provided in the Question/Answer booklet.

*In the passage which follows, the travel writer, Jan Morris, describes her impressions of Aberdeen in the early 1980s.*

# Oil on Granite

1    For my tastes the harbour of Aberdeen is marvellous to see in the evening.  It is not a big harbour, two artificial inlets attached to the mouth of the Dee and protected by a breakwater against the open sea, but it is always in motion.  The rusty flotillas of fishing-boats may be asleep, their blur of masts and funnels illuminated only by a few masthead lights, but the oil docks all around are brilliantly awake.  The tall storage tanks glitter in the floodlights.  The ungainly supply-boats, humped up forward, elongated aft, hum at their quays.  From the shrouded shape of a vessel in the yards, towered over by derricks, a fireworks spray of oxy-acetylene showers through the dusk.

2    There are hissing, clanging and thumping noises, the pilot launch scuds here and there, the hulk of a freighter heaves itself cautiously from a quay, the Orkney steamer slips away down the navigation channel, exchanging incomprehensible Scotticisms with the harbourmen in their tower.  Out at sea four or five supply-boats lie beneath their riding lights, and sometimes a helicopter comes clanking in from the east, heavily over the docks towards the airport.

3    Aberdeen is the chief support base for the North Sea oil operations.  Here are the supply-ships, the depots, the aircraft, the electronics, the technical agencies, which sustain the storm-battered rigs and platforms far out at sea.  Thousands of millions of pounds are invested in these craft and machineries; skills from a dozen nations are concentrated here;  through this conduit Americans, Englishmen, Frenchmen, Dutchmen, Spaniards, Italians, Greeks, Norwegians, Swedes, Germans, pass in a ceaseless traffic to and from the oilfields out of sight.

4    Yet behind the harbour, as night falls, the city of Aberdeen stands grave and grey.  A tower or two, of kirk or civic pile, stand sentinel beyond the cranes, like keepers of the public conscience, but there are no skyscrapers, revolving restaurants on towers, neon lights or blazing late-night stores.  No thump of disco echoes down Mill Brae or Rennies Wynd.  Aberdeen seems hardly more than a backdrop to the performance on its own quays, for though this old and respected burgh has long joined the list of boom towns, Kimberley to Abu Dhabi, it remains tentative to the experience.  Other towns have gold rushes or silver strikes:  Aberdeen's is a distinctly granite bonanza.

5    Handsome, civilized, diligent, granite, Aberdeen has never been rich before, but has always been canny.  Until the oil strikes it lived by fishing and agriculture, and though it knew much poverty and unemployment in the bad old days, it never let its standards slip.  Its very substance seemed indestructible, so that its buildings never looked either old or new, never particularly shabby, never noticeably opulent.

6    It is very hard to date a building in Aberdeen, so easily does one century blend into the next. The grandest houses in town, the severe granite villas built for the trawler-owners at the turn of the century, are scarcely ostentatious: the old fishing quarter of Footdee, jumbled on the shore beside the harbour, is still occupied by fishing families and dockyard workers, but has been done up bijou-style by the council, with concrete bowls for shrubberies, and dainty cobbled yards.

7    This city of 200,000 lies halfway between Edinburgh and John O'Groats. Here the produce of the eastern Highlands traditionally comes to market, here the fish of the north are frozen, whisked away to London or turned into malodorous by-products. Aberdeen is deeply rooted.

8    Little has really changed since the 18th century, I would imagine, at the auction by which, each morning at 8 am, the trawlers dispose of their catch. The boats, rimmed still with frost and ice from the fishing grounds, mostly look antique themselves, and the fishermen look altogether timeless, stalwart, comely men, their faces rigid in the truest Scottish mould, unhurried, polite; and there the fish of the cold seas lie as they always did, cod, hake and flatfish, glistening in their wooden crates. Through all the hub-bub, the slithering of seaboots, the clattering of boxes, the chugging of engines, the shrieking of seabirds, the slurping of tea from enamel mugs, white-coated auctioneers immemorially grunt their prices, and lorries rumble away over the cobbled quays.

9    It is an interesting but not an exhilarating scene, but then Aberdeen is not built for exuberance. It is not, as one of its inhabitants remarked to me, a *fizzy* town.

10    The crime rate is the lowest, as are the juvenile delinquency rate, and the vandalism rate, and the unemployment rate: and the educational standards are the highest, and the long beach promenade is entirely unvulgarized, and the town has won the Britain in Bloom contest so often that it has tactfully withdrawn from the contest. Aberdeen has an enterprising arts centre, municipally supported, and its high-rise buildings have been tastefully held in check, and its industrial development is discreetly zoned, and altogether it is in many ways the best of all possible burghs.

11    Upon this hoary and provident town the bonanza of oil has fallen more or less out of the sky. Until I went to Aberdeen I had no conception of its scale. Seen against so stolid a setting, it is staggering. One oil person actually apologised to me for a development that cost a mere million: anything less than a billion or two is hardly worth mentioning. There is nothing modest to the North Sea oil affair.

12    It is like a war, and billeted upon Aberdeen, as alien to the city as the officers of some occupying army, are the staffs and technical corps of the campaign. This is the intelligence base of the North Sea operations, the logistical centre, the technical depot: here too are all the auxiliaries, financiers to camp followers, landladies to economists. The local oil directory lists them all, and their very entries on the page are like a roll-call of regiments, drawn from all corners of some great alliance, and assembled beneath their several flags in this unlikely outpost.

13    But there is beauty here. It is the beauty of power and innovation, which inspired the artist Turner in his day, but is hard to find in modern Britain. It is the brutal beauty of competitive enterprise: men racing each other, the snatch for profit, the outpouring of colossal resources in the hope of still more immense returns. It suits this hard northern coastline, where the wild storms sweep in from the sea, and where once the Aberdeen clippers sailed out to capture the prizes of the tea trade. Oil tycoons may have their doubts about London, even about Edinburgh, but they can hardly quarrel with Aberdeen.

Adapted from *Journeys* by Jan Morris

*[END OF PASSAGE]*

## QUESTIONS

### Write your answers in the spaces provided.

**Look at Paragraphs 1 and 2.**

1. (a) Explain, **in your own words**, why the writer thinks that Aberdeen harbour is "marvellous to see in the evening".

there is always things happening, all
the boats are in the harbour

2 ■ 0

(b) **Write down two** expressions in the passage which support your answer to Question 1 (a).

2 1 0

(i) "always in motion"

(ii) "flotillas of fishing boat may be asleep"

2. Explain fully why you think the writer describes the fishing-boats' masts and funnels as a "blur".

as the masts are so tall that it is
hard to see the tops.

2 1 0

3. Explain clearly, **in your own words**, what it is about the supply-boats that the writer finds "ungainly".

2 1 0

4. Why are the Scotticisms described as "incomprehensible"?

2 ■ 0

*Marks*

5. In Paragraph 2, the writer describes the movement of three different boats. Explain fully why any **one** of these descriptions is particularly effective.

_____

_____

_____

_____

2 | 1 | 0

**Look at Paragraph 4.**

6. The "city of Aberdeen stands grave and grey". Explain clearly how the writer continues these **two** descriptions of the city in this paragraph.

grave + grey as there is no skyscrapers,
resturants or towers etc.

_____

_____

2 | 1 | 0

7. Aberdeen "remains tentative to the experience". **In your own words**, say to what "experience" the writer is referring.

that this was the best Aberdeen
could do and have done in past years
but still they enjoy it.

2 | 1 | 0

**Look at Paragraph 5.**

8. The writer uses the word "granite" to refer not only to the stone used in Aberdeen, but to a quality she feels the city has. **Write down** an expression which repeats the idea of that quality.

"Canny" + "indestructible"

2 | ■ | 0

9. The writer states that Aberdeen's buildings are "never noticeably opulent". Which expression in Paragraph 6 repeats this idea?

"are scarely noticeable"

2 | ■ | 0

*Marks*

**Look at Paragraph 7.**

**10.** Explain clearly how the writer shows that Aberdeen is a long-established city.

with markets, with fish caught from
sea and highland produce also being
sold

2 ■ 0

**Look at Paragraph 8.**

**11.** The writer imagines that "little has really changed" at the daily auction since the 18th century.

**Write down two** words or expressions which support this idea.

2 1 0

(i) _____

(ii) _____

**12.** By close reference to the final sentence of Paragraph 8, show how the writer creates the impression of a "hub-bub" at the auction:

(*a*) by word choice;

_____

_____

_____

2 1 0

(*b*) by sentence structure.

_____

_____

_____

2 1 0

Marks

**Look at Paragraph 10.**

13. The writer calls Aberdeen "the best of all possible burghs". In Paragraph 5, she says it is "handsome, civilized, diligent".

**Write down one** piece of information from Paragraph 10 which relates to each of these words.

2 1 0

Handsome  "new buildings being built"

Civilized  "crime is at the lowest rate"

Diligent  _____

14. (a) What is unusual about the sentence structure of Paragraph 10?

_____

_____

2 ■ 0

(b) What effect do you think the writer hopes to achieve by this structure?

_____

_____

2 ■ 0

**Look at Paragraph 11.**

15. "There is nothing modest to the North Sea oil affair."

Explain, **in your own words**, how the earlier part of the paragraph helps you to understand this sentence.

as ~~oil~~ oil is such a big industry

and on such a Big scale.

_____

2 1 0

*Marks*

**Look at Paragraph 12.**

16. The writer says that the oil business is "like a war".

   (*a*) **Write down three** words or expressions which continue this idea.

   2  1  0

   (i) "Officers of some occupying army"

   (ii) "intelligance base'

   (iii) "technical corps"

   (*b*) Explain clearly how **one** of your answers to Question 16(*a*) compares the oil business to a war.

   ii) as each company had a base to plan and exicute there plans.

   2  1  0

**Look at Paragraph 13.**

17. (*a*) Explain, **in your own words**, what, according to the writer, is "the brutal beauty of competitive enterprise".

   it was like a game, everyone trying to get as much oil as possible.

   2  1  0

   (*b*) Explain clearly how the writer shows that "competitive enterprise" is not new to Aberdeen.

   2  1  0

**Think about the passage as a whole.**

18. In what way does the title reflect the author's attitude to Aberdeen?
(Your answer should refer **in some detail** to the content of the passage.)

_Marks_

_____

_____

_____

_____

_____

| 2 | 1 | 0 |

*[END OF QUESTION PAPER]*

SCOTTISH
CERTIFICATE OF
EDUCATION
1995

WEDNESDAY, 3 MAY
2.30 PM – 3.20 PM

# ENGLISH
## STANDARD GRADE
Credit Level

Reading

Text

Read carefully the passage.  It will help if you read it twice.  When you have done so, answer the questions.
Use the spaces provided in the Question/Answer booklet.

*In the extract which follows, a young boy, Howard, lies to his father and learns a
lesson.*

1    On winter evenings he fed the cows after the milking, pushing between them with
armfuls of hay.  They were tethered to the stalls loosely by chains round their necks
but he had to mind the points of the horns as they turned with their soft eyes, sweet
breath and rasping tongues curled delicately out for the hay.

2    It was 1910 and Howard was a year older than the century.  They had the small
farm of Burnfoot where they grew oats and potatoes and reared a few sheep and the
cows on whom they mainly depended.

3    In the mornings he helped his mother and father with the milking;  when the milk
was cooled it went into the big metal churns.  The cows, about a dozen depending on
how many had calved at the time, gave enough milk to fill three churns a day, and
they were taken to the Creamery in Lanark.

4    On Saturdays and in the holidays it might be Howard who took them, in a cart
pulled by a big white bony horse.  Ever since he'd been old enough to do this there
had been days when an aeroplane droned over like a wasp, low because it would be
going to land at the Racecourse;  he would see the man's head and might get a wave
of his leather-gauntleted hand, but he didn't wave back.  The aviators weren't
ordinary people;  their photographs were in the paper sometimes.  They belonged in
papers.  He got on with the job, thinking his own thoughts and watching the backside
of the horse and hearing the heavy chinking of the churns.

5    If he went by the top road he'd sometimes see the planes on the Racecourse,
though never going up or coming down, as if they did that in secret.

6    "They're asking for trouble," his father said, his big legs folded at the table, the
tackets in his boots squealing shortly when he moved—ready to stride out if anything
was wrong—his moustache bristling over the paper.  "They'll catch it," he'd add.  In
the early days of aviation his father detested its uselessness and looked for the flyers
to get their come-uppance.  And being superstitious he was certain they'd get it that
very year, the year of Halley's Comet.  But when the clear May nights came and they
saw the Comet passing over, no disasters had struck the Lanark flyers.  The world
went on as usual;  other people joked about the old notion that the Comet brought
bad luck.  In the farmhouse his father went on insisting they'd get their deserts
sooner or later—because they flew in the air, boldly challenging the stars, Howard
supposed, although he felt that his father was dead set against them for more reasons
than that.

7    On Saturday 11 August they staged an international competition with contestants from England, France and the United States. Coming back the Racecourse way from the Creamery, he saw planes of every colour in front of the grandstand. Going among them were the aviators, shouting and laughing. He stopped the cart. They were ordinary people, but different from anyone he'd met in Lanark. He remembered a group of bicyclists he'd met on the road once, men and women in strange clothes. They'd greeted him as they passed, friendly but entirely different. He'd stared without answering but days later was excited to have been, it seemed, equals on the road. The aviators were something similar . . . he trotted the horse home, the empty churns bouncing in the cart, and said he was going back up the road for brambles.

8    His father looked at the sweating horse, and after a pause he said that that would be alright. Howard could see he knew the berries weren't ready yet, like the ones behind the steading that they always picked; and he understood that this was a lesson being set up for him when he came home without brambles: not to tell lies. And there'd be another lesson behind this one, the real lesson: that his father had been right about that sort of new-fangled nonsense coming to grief.

9    In spite of this, he forgot it all and slipped through the Racecourse fence.

10    A crowd mobbed around the grandstand where they served drinks and sandwiches. He made his way through the high society of Lanark, dolled up to the nines and mingled with noisy, alarming foreigners. He wished he hadn't come. Then as no-one paid any attention to him, he wandered out among the planes. They were fragile and dazzling, the opposites of the solid farm carts. Sometimes the aviator would be sitting in the cockpit while a mechanic tried the plane's propeller. In others the mechanics tuned the engines. The air was full of roaring, the strange exciting smell of gasoline, and drawling voices talking of their kites.

11    He found himself beside a yellow plane. A man in the cockpit, in ordinary cap and glasses, looked straight at him through the thick lenses. "Hey, will you lend me a hand?" he called in a kind voice. His plane was as yellow as scrambled eggs.

12    Howard hesitated. "Yes," he said at last.

13    The man asked him to hold a bolt on the outside while he tightened the nut inside the fuselage. It was done in a moment. "That's it!" he shouted cheerily when it was fixed.

14    "I hope you win," Howard said.

15    "Thanks, my boy!" shouted the aviator above the roar of the engines, "Keep your fingers crossed for me! Number 24!"

16    There was shouting through a loudspeaker, increased roaring of the engines, throbbing of planes, a movement of the crowd to get the best places on the rails, people running in their fashionable clothes. He ran too, dodging through them to the blackboard beside the grandstand. He read: "24—Mr Cecil Grace—Farman monoplane".

17    The heavy, powerful roar of engines increased though it had already seemed as loud as it could be; the planes rolled at intervals across the turf and took off as lightly as flies.

18    24! Still wearing cap and glasses as if he was going for a walk, he lined up for his turn. You could see it was just pure fun for him. He waved—to someone special it seemed—and moved to the start of his take-off. Howard was anxious. This man might be the target of his father's prediction and the Comet's bad luck. He was too happy.

19    The yellow plane wafted up as if carried by a gust of air and circled higher and higher among the rest.  The sky was full of planes like birds, circling and getting smaller.  Howard was dizzy from looking up.  He couldn't tell which was number 24 any more, they were too high, but the yellow plane was in his thoughts so much that he feared to see it falling from the sky, twisting and spinning.  He felt the fear in his legs and ran from the Racecourse.

20    The paper carried the result later in the week.  Mr Grace had been fifth.  He was alright!  And now Howard saw him distinctly when he'd landed, handing over his kite to the mechanic, smiling, moving in a slow easy way, short-sighted in the glasses.

21    There had been no accidents at all.  He began thinking that his father could be wrong—a gradual process;  the thought had been in his mind some time before he acknowledged it.  He grew used to it then, but as a single instance, not affecting the rest of his father's enormous rightness.

Adapted from *The Aviators* by John Cunningham

[END OF PASSAGE]

## QUESTIONS

**Write your answers in the spaces provided.**

**Look at Paragraphs 1 to 3.**

1. (a) **Write down two** expressions the writer uses to describe the cows' more attractive features.

   (i) _Soft eyes_

   (ii) _Sweet breath_

   (b) **Write down two** expressions which suggest the cows' less agreeable features.

   (i) _points on horns_

   (ii) _rasping tongues_

2. (a) How old was Howard?

   _10 11 years old_

   (b) Why does the writer choose to express his age in this way?

   _____

   _____

3. "... the cows on whom they mainly depended."
   Explain clearly how the writer reinforces their importance to the family.

   _'gave enough milk to fill the churns three times a day._

   _____

*Marks*

**Look at Paragraph 4.**

4. An aviator might wave to Howard "but he didn't wave back".

   (a) Explain fully, **in your own words**, HOW Howard did react.

   *He couldn't wave as he was controlling the horses with his hands*

   | 2 | 1 | 0 |

   (b) Explain fully, **in your own words**, WHY Howard reacted in this way.

   *as Howard thinks aviators aren't ordinary people*

   | 2 | 1 | 0 |

**Look at Paragraph 6.**

5. ". . . his moustache bristling over the paper."
   Why is "bristling" a particularly appropriate word to use in this context?

   *ready for action*

   | 2 | 1 | 0 |

6. Howard's father expected "the flyers to get their come-uppance".
   Which expression later in the paragraph repeats this idea?

   *'they'd get their deserts sooner or later'*

   | 2 | ■ | 0 |

7. **In your own words** say what Howard supposed his father's reasons were for being against the aviators.

   *he though that there was more reasons than his father had said*

   | 2 | 1 | 0 |

**Look at Paragraph 7.**

8. What made Howard stop the cart on this occasion?

   *that he had seen ordinary people, but different from anyone else he had met in Lanark*

   | 2 | 1 | 0 |

*Marks*

9. "The aviators were something similar . . ."
   In what ways did Howard think they were similar to the bicyclists?

   friendly but entirely different

   | 2 | 1 | 0 |

10. Which sentence indicates a change in Howard's attitude to the aviators?

    The aviators were something...

    | 2 | ■ | 0 |

**Look at Paragraph 8.**

11. How could Howard tell from his father's hesitation that "this was a lesson . . . not to tell lies"?

    because Howard ~~had~~ might ~~of~~ have
    seen this look before from his dad

    | 2 | 1 | 0 |

12. **In your own words**, explain what Howard's father expected the "real lesson" to be.

    planes + aviators wouldn't work

    | 2 | 1 | 0 |

**Look at Paragraph 9.**

13. Explain how this one-sentence paragraph is an effective link between Paragraphs 8 and 10.

    father → busy

    | 2 | 1 | 0 |

**Look at Paragraph 10.**

14. Explain, **in your own words**, why Howard "wished he hadn't come".

    as the place was loud and busy.
    and was full of foreingers

    | 2 | 1 | 0 |

51

*Marks*

**15.** "... he wandered out among the planes."

    (*a*) **Quote two** expressions from the rest of this paragraph which convey Howard's sense of wonder.

        (i) _dazziling_

        (ii) _drawling voices_

**2 1 0**

    (*b*) Explain how **one** of these expressions highlights the contrast with Howard's everyday life.

        _dazziling and fragile_

**2 1 0**

**Look at Paragraph 16.**

**16.** (*a*) What impression does the writer wish to convey in the first sentence?

        _That it was starting to get lively and exciting_

**2 1 0**

    (*b*) Explain **two** ways in which the sentence structure contributes to this impression.

**2 1 0**

        (i) _roaring of engines_

        (ii) _throbbing of planes_

**17.** Why didn't Howard run to the rails with the crowd?

    _he went to the blackboard_

**2 1 0**

Marks

**Look at Paragraph 18.**

18. "You could see it was just pure fun for him."

    Give **two** pieces of evidence to support this statement.

    2 1 0

    (i) _as if he was still going for a walk_

    (ii) _he waved_

19. Explain, **in your own words**, why Howard was anxious.

    _in case his fathers prediction was_
    _to come true._

    2 1 0

**Look at Paragraph 21.**

20. Which expression illustrates the real lesson that Howard has learned?

    _He had been thinking his_

    _father could be wrong_

    2 ■ 0

**Think about the passage as a whole.**

21. What does the final sentence add to your understanding of the changing relationship between Howard and his father?

    _That Howard had learned to not_
    _take in some of the thing that_
    _his father predicts_

    2 1 0

[*END OF QUESTION PAPER*]

SCOTTISH
CERTIFICATE OF
EDUCATION
1996

TUESDAY, 7 MAY
2.30 PM – 3.20 PM

ENGLISH
STANDARD GRADE
Credit Level
Reading
Text

Read carefully the passage. It will help if you read it twice. When you have done so, answer the questions. Use the spaces provided in the Question/Answer booklet.

*This passage is an extract from a novel set in Russia in 1905.  It describes a childhood experience of an encounter with death.*

1 Asya pulled on her coat and boots, closed the pantry door and slipped away before anyone saw her disappear.  Her breath streamed through her muffler and rose up into the birch branches above her head. The icicles on the eaves shed a steady stream of drops into the piled snowbanks on either side of the path;  clumps of snow slid off the branches of the firs and subsided to the ground with a hiss; the uppermost branches of the birches sighed and cracked in the wind.  She skipped down the hundred and twenty-six wooden steps to the boathouse singing to herself.

2 Inside the boathouse, slivers of winter light streamed through the gaps between the plank walls and sliced her body into planes of illumination and darkness.  The racing craft gleamed on the rafters above her head and the motor launch, suspended above its river berth by twin ropes, swayed slightly to and fro, making a dry, creaking sound.

3 She climbed down the boathouse ladder and tested the ice with her boot.  Then she pushed open the great wooden doors and stepped out into the fierce light of the silver river.  In the far distance, she could just make out the thin line of the opposite shore.  Father had once crossed the river on snowshoes.  She would too.  She would astonish them all.  She walked along, sucking her mitten.

4 She glanced back at the house, where she had left her brother Lapin playing snakes and ladders with Nanny Saunders, but the village of Marino had vanished in the mist.  Whenever she stopped pushing her boots through the slushy ice, she could hear the river roaring beneath her feet.  Soon the ice would begin to heave and crack, and the air would fill with a groaning sound as if the whole earth were in pain.  Then the river would throw off its mantle and jagged chunks would begin to shift and then bob past the dock.  She loved it when the frozen world began to move, when the torrent of life reclaimed the river for its own.  Marino would awaken from its sleep. The boatman would sand and revarnish the hull of the motor launch and grease the oarlocks on the rowing boat.  As soon as the ice was off the water, Father would dive naked from the boathouse and roar when he surfaced, throwing the hair out of his eyes.

5 She slopped through the slush, thinking of Spring.  By the time she reached the middle of the river, the mist had enveloped her.  The boathouse behind her was gone, and the long, smudged line of her water-filled steps trailed away into nothingness.  The pencil line of the opposite shore had disappeared.  She stood still and listened.  A faint sound. A scythe being drawn against a sharpening-stone.  A blade being honed on something hard.  She turned around, sucking her mitten, trying to figure out which direction the sound was coming from.  Blades scything, blades hissing, coming closer.  Where had she heard that sound before?  Then she knew.  It was a skater, out there in the mist, coming towards her.  No one she knew.

They were all inside. She could hear his breathing now, his body at full stretch, his blades slicing into the river's skin. She stood still, waiting for him, unafraid and alone. The veil of mist burst apart, the vast white figure hurtled past her and the ice beneath her feet gave way. She subsided into a dark hole of water, clutching at the jagged rim, while the river seized hold of her and tore her boots from her feet. The river roared in her ears and liquid warmth—like that of a nursery bath—rose through her body and she let herself be swept away.

6    Then faces were leaning over her, and hands were busy about her, rubbing her limbs frantically, wiping the tears from their faces with such a look of desolation that she wanted to ask what the matter was, but could not speak, only stare up at them from the warm watery place where she had gone. She was borne aloft and carried upwards, wrapped up tight, as if in swaddling. From where she lay in their arms, she stared up into the black, naked branches of trees lit by the pink sky of dusk. Beneath her and behind her she could hear the steady crunch of boots in the snow and a woman weeping. She could not move her head or see where she was being taken.

7    She opened her eyes and saw that Praskoviya was bathing her face with a cloth. How much better it had been out on the river. How much better it had been in the warm, watery place. How beautiful their tears had seemed when she could only lie there and watch them fall. How painful they were now, when you could reach up and wipe them from Praskoviya's face.

8    "My child! You have come back from the dead! The Lord be praised."

9    Why was she talking of death? There was no death on the river, only warmth suffusing her body and the certainty of having seen a great vision.

10    "Whatever possessed you, my dearest?" Her mother's voice, close by, gentle, anguished.

11    Her eyes shut tight, Asya heard herself say in a shrill voice: "I saw a skater. A great skater. Out there. On the ice."

12    She looked up. They were all crowded around her bed: Father, Mother, her brother Lapin, Praskoviya, but she could tell from their faces that no one had seen what she had seen or heard what she had heard. All the remaining years of her life, she remembered that moment: (when she discovered the abyss of unknowing that separated her from those she loved.)

13    She looked about her. Where was Nanny Saunders?

14    Her father laid his hand upon hers.

15    "The groom is accompanying her to the station."

16    "But why?"

17    "She has been dismissed for letting you out of her sight."

18    All the way back to England? In the winter? She could imagine the black carriage trotting through the dark woods, Nanny Saunders with her boxes in the back seat.

19    "Don't cry, child, don't cry."

20    But there was no stopping these tears, mixed with grief and rage. Much later, when she had learned what life was like, she remembered this as the moment when she discovered injustice, and the possibility that a father could be responsible for it.

21    "It was not Nanny's fault. You told me you crossed the river. It's not her fault! Call her back!"

22    Dr Feldman tried to force her head back onto the pillow. "You mustn't, child, you mustn't . . ."

23    "I cannot call her back. My mind is made up," said Father in that reasonable tone of voice that she knew issued from a will stronger than her own.

24    "But you told me you crossed the river on snowshoes."

25    "Did I, child?" His long face with its neatly trimmed beard, smelling of wintergreen, was close to hers. She could not bear to think that he had forgotten, that he took his words to her so lightly. She turned away from her father and began to cry.

Adapted from *Asya* by Michael Ignatieff

*[END OF PASSAGE]*

**QUESTIONS**

**Write your answers in the spaces provided.**

**Look at Paragraph 1.**

1. **Write down** an expression which suggests that Asya went out secretly.

   *"Slipped away before anyone saw her disappear"*

   2 ■ 0

2. **In your own words**, give **two** pieces of evidence that there was a thaw.

   (i) _____

   (ii) _____

   2 1 0

3. (*a*) What kind of mood did Asya seem to be in?

   *happy, jolly*

   2 ■ 0

   (*b*) Write down **two** separate words which the writer uses to convey the impression of her mood.

   | singing | | skipped |

   2 1 0

**Look at Paragraph 2.**

4. **Using your own words**, describe the effect of the winter light on Asya's appearance.

   *The light split her in half with patches of lights all over her body.*

   2 1 0

Marks

**Look at Paragraph 3.**

5. Asya "stepped out into the fierce light of the silver river".

   (a) Explain clearly why the light would seem "fierce".

   the light was powerful, <sup>almost</sup> blinding

   her

   |2|1|0|

   (b) Give **two** reasons why you think the writer chose the word "silver" to describe the river.

   |2|1|0|

   (i) shiney, reflective

   (ii) _____

6. How does the writer convey the idea that Asya was determined, yet seemed nervous, about crossing the river?

   |2|1|0|

   Determined  "She would too", "She would

   astonish them all"

   Nervous  sucking her mitten

**Look at Paragraphs 4 and 5.**

7. **In your own words**, describe the **three** things Asya looked forward to once the ice had gone.

   |2|1|0|

   (i) the town would start to be more lively

   (ii) being able to do things with her father

   (iii) seeing the boatman doing his jobs

8. "She slopped through the slush . . ."

   How is the writer's choice of words effective in describing Asya walking across the river?

   she didn't put much effort in.  The

   surface was wet and like mush

   |2|1|0|

*Marks*

9. "... the mist had enveloped her."

Explain **in your own words** how the writer develops this idea in the two sentences which follow.

*everything had disappeared all around her, even the faintest things had dissappeared. She was all alone*

2 | 1 | 0

10. "She stood still and listened."

   (*a*) What **two** features of structure does the writer use to convey the sound Asya hears?

   2 | 1 | 0

   (i) *one after another*

   (ii) _____

   (*b*) Why does he choose to write in this way?

   _____

   _____

   2 | 1 | 0

11. (*a*) What impression of the skater is created by the writer's description?

   *mystical*

   2 | ■ | 0

   (*b*) **Quote** an expression to support your answer to question 11(*a*).

   *"the vast white figure"*

   2 | ■ | 0

12. Why does the expression "... his blades slicing into the river's skin" suggest a sense of danger?

   *like a knife – "blades into the (rivers) skin.*

   2 | 1 | 0

Marks

13. "... liquid warmth—"

"—like that of a nursery bath—"

(a) Given the context, what is surprising about these two expressions?

    (i) *that the nursery baths were as cold as icey water.*

    (ii) *how ice and warm can be used together in the same sentence*

2 | 1 | 0

(b) Which expressions in **Paragraph 6** continue these unusual ideas?

    (i) *"warm watery place"*

    (ii) _____

2 | 1 | 0

14. The writer describes the river as if it were a living thing.

(a) Give an example of this.

*"the river seized hold of her and tore her boots from her feet"*

2 | ■ | 0

(b) Comment on the effect of your chosen example.

*it gives an empresion of a person doing this.*

2 | 1 | 0

**Look at Paragraph 6.**

15. Why might the people's faces have had "such a look of desolation"?

*as they thought she might be dead*

2 | ■ | 0

**Look at Paragraphs 7 to 9.**

16. "My child! You have come back from the dead! The Lord be praised."

Explain why Asya was puzzled when she heard this.

*She didn't know what was going on and understand what she meant by "dead"*

2 | 1 | 0

*Marks*

**Look at Paragraphs 10 to 12.**

17. **In your own words**, explain what Asya remembered about that moment "all the remaining years of her life".

_____

_____ 2 ■ 0

**Look at Paragraphs 13 to 25.**

18. Explain clearly why Asya felt it was "not Nanny's fault".

as Asya had sneaked out so that
no one would of heard her. 2 1 0

19. In these final paragraphs of the passage, Asya learned things about her father which disappointed her.

Describe **two** of them as fully as you can.

(i) that her father had made the Nanny
leave to go home all the way to England
in winter. 2 1 0

(ii) That the father hadn't spoken to
Asya first. 2 1 0

**Think about the passage as a whole.**

20. There are several important moments for Asya in this extract.

(a) Which **one** do you think affected her most?

That her father let her down.

_____ 2 ■ 0

(b) **By close reference to the passage**, explain your choice as fully as you can.

He hadn't consulted Asya and had
just fired her on the spot. And making
her return home in winter. 2 1 0

*[END OF QUESTION PAPER]*

SCOTTISH
CERTIFICATE OF
EDUCATION
1997

WEDNESDAY, 7 MAY
2.30 PM – 3.20 PM

ENGLISH
STANDARD GRADE
Credit Level
Reading
Text

Read carefully the passage. It will help if you read it twice. When you have done so, answer the questions. Use the spaces provided in the Question/Answer booklet.

# That old white magic of Wicca's world

**The ancient pagan religion of witchcraft (or "Wicca") has not always been perceived as evil. However the craft has suffered from a prolonged spell of bad publicity.**

The devil's daughters: James VI took witchcraft so seriously that he wrote a treatise against it, personally supervised the torture of witches, and blamed a coven in North Berwick, shown in this contemporary woodcut, for a storm at sea in which he was caught in 1590.

1 PITY the poor witch on Hallowe'en as she climbs aboard her trusty broomstick and, with familiar cat riding pillion, whizzes off to the *Samhain Sabbat*. She has had an awfully bad press over the years.

2 In popular folklore, she is the warty old crone who dances naked around a bonfire on the nights of the eight annual sabbats and then, as dawn breaks, smears herself with "flying ointment" and jets back home for a glass of toadslime and a hot bath.

3 She is the old dear forever depicted as a somewhat unlovely woman dressed casually in black and wearing an ungainly pointy bunnet. Let's face it, looking like that she would stick out a mile in your average supermarket.

4 Our perceptions of the witchcraft cult are deeply and subconsciously rooted: we may scoff at childhood terrors, but how many of us would be entirely happy walking through a graveyard at night? We may have forgotten our fear of the dark and the supernatural, but we have also seen *Nightmare on Elm Street*.

5 The witch has come to symbolise primordial fears lurking just beneath the surface in all of us: Freddie, *Night of the Living Dead*, and the bogeyman rolled into one. The three witches in *Macbeth*, prancing and cackling around their cauldron, provide the accepted clichés on witch behaviour and taste:

> *Eye of newt, and toe of frog*
> *Wool of bat, and tongue of dog*
> *Adder's fork, and blind-worm's*
> *sting*
> *Lizard's leg and howlet's wing*

6 However "tongue of dog" and "adder's fork" are plants—the former

used as the basis for a contemporary cough medicine. Shakespeare, living as he was at the beginning of the great witch persecutions, perhaps was not above pulling a few legs. Alas, the *Macbeth* witches have merely served to reinforce prejudice, rather than cast illumination.

7   So does the witch deserve her poor image? As she frolics cold and naked, invoking the names of the old gods — Cernunnos and the moon goddess Diana — might it not occur to her that over the centuries she has had a pretty raw deal? In many ways, she would be quite right.

8   It is probable that the Wiccan creed goes back to the dawn of religious belief, when cave dwellers peered out and saw wonder in the rhythm of the changing seasons. Early cave drawings from across Europe — and elsewhere — show remarkable similarities, particularly in their depiction of a horned god.

9   Early witchcraft was probably no more than a primitive attempt to make sense of the unknown. It is likely that the Wiccan horned god was an earlier version of the Greek god Pan. So how come this religion became associated with hubble bubble, toil and trouble?

10   The answer was an unhappy alliance between the spread of Christianity and social upheaval. In the so-called Dark Ages witchcraft was considered no more than a misdemeanour, warranting the equivalent of community service; yet in the "enlightened" Renaissance, the fires burned across Europe (except in England where witchcraft was a hanging offence).

11   During the 15th century, witchcraft and Christianity had co-existed; the church recognising that older pagan cults of beliefs could not easily be repressed — particularly in backward rural communities where survival was often a matter of luck, and old superstitions die hard.

12   The book *Malleus Maleficarum* (*Hammer of the Witches*), published in 1486, was the trigger for a change in attitude which gave the Church the big stick it needed to beat non-conformity and heresy; in the process, it sparked a Europe-wide holocaust against Jew and witch alike. (In some areas of Europe, the *Malleus* was used specifically against Jews; indeed, in Hungary a first offender found guilty of witchcraft was made to stand for a day in a public place wearing a Jew's hat.)

13   In England, where judicial torture was illegal (except for some treasonable crimes), the witch persecution was mild compared to elsewhere in Europe. In Scotland, however, judicial torture was practised with uncommon zeal; for example, the use of pennywinkis which crushed the toes and fingers, or the leg screw which splintered the shin bone. Small wonder that the victim confessed and, having done so, named her accomplices. The beauty of the witch craze was that it was self-fulfilling; the more brightly the witch fires burned, the more victims were then found.

14   In Scotland, the first witch law in 1563 prescribed the death penalty for all witches, "good" and "bad". Until then the Church had made a distinction between harmless superstitious belief and what might now be termed black magic — a distinction that modern witches see as fundamental to an understanding of their belief

15   Thereafter, all witchcraft was evil — James VI of Scotland also abolished the distinction in England on his accession to the throne there — and the black-hatted old crone as modern stereotype begins to emerge. One aspect of that stereotype is true: it was women who bore the brunt of it. One estimate suggests one hundred women died for every man condemned for witchcraft.

16   The simple explanation is that local wisewomen offered an easy target. Since time immemorial, these local worthies had acted as doctor, vet, pharmacist and midwife, offering an accumulation of folk wisdom handed down over the generations. During the years of persecution, it became a job with few prospects when anyone with a score to settle could denounce the wisewoman as a witch.

17   The persecution may be behind us but the witches live on. Estimates of their numbers are understandably hard to find but the upsurge in the number of (white witch) covens reflects both a disenchantment with modern technological life and a desire to return to more primitive roots — the religious equivalent of herbal healthcare.

18   Witchcraft echoes still abound in petty superstition — for example, the number 13 (the number of witches in a coven), or throwing salt over our left shoulder. And how many people know that the children's rhyme *Who Killed Cock Robin?* is a reference to the now-defunct English Wiccan ritual of sacrificing small birds in the apple orchards?

19   Nowadays your average witch is likely to be called Harry or Morag and live in a nice wee house in the country or a council flat in town. On the way to the *Samhain Sabbat*, he/she is also likely to go by bus or car, rather than risk it on the carpet shampooer (technology again, you see). And no, she won't take a short-cut home through the graveyard. Like you and I, she would be too frightened.

Adapted from an article in *The Scotsman* by Charles Laidlaw

*[END OF PASSAGE]*

## QUESTIONS

**Write your answers in the spaces provided.**

**Look at Paragraphs 1 to 3.**

1. **In your own words**, give **three** pieces of information which are popularly believed about witches.

    (i) _there cats fly with them._

    (ii) _they dance naked around a bonfire_

    (iii) _they then smear 'flying ointment' on themselves then fly hom._

2|1|0

**Look at Paragraphs 4 to 6.**

2. "Our perceptions of the witchcraft cult are deeply and subconsciously rooted".

    (*a*) What **two** examples does the writer give in Paragraph 4 to support this idea?

    _even the _____ (( ____ we still_

    _subconser_

2|1|0

    (*b*) Which expression in Paragraph 5 contains a similar idea to this quotation?

2|1|0

3. In what way does the quotation from *Macbeth* show that Shakespeare was "pulling a few legs"?

    _as some of the ingredients were fake, some were plants used for medicine_

2|1|0

4. Explain **in your own words** any **one** belief the writer has about the *Macbeth* witches.

    _that they were made up, fake they were uses to continue the idea of witches._

2|1|0

Marks

**Look at Paragraph 7.**

5. In what way can Paragraph 7 be regarded as a link of the ideas within the article?

> As it gives a summary of the article so far.

2 | 1 | 0

**Look at Paragraphs 8 and 9.**

6. **Quote** an expression which shows that the writer is not certain of the facts.

> "It is likely that..."

2 | ■ | 0

7. **In your own words**, explain what the writer believes was the purpose of early witchcraft.

> an attempt to understand this that were unknown before

2 | 1 | 0

8. What is the difference in tone between the last sentence of Paragraph 9 and the rest of these two paragraphs?

> The tone is unsure, it is asking a question

2 | ■ | 0

**Look at Paragraphs 10 to 12.**

9. Explain **in your own words** how you can tell that witchcraft wasn't badly thought of in the Dark Ages.

> as it didn't have as big a punishment as later years, witchcraft + christianity both existed and noticed

2 | 1 | 0

10. Why has the writer used inverted commas round the word "enlightened"?

> people know knew about it.

2 | 1 | 0

*Marks*

**11.** **In your own words**, explain clearly why the Christian Church accepted the existence of witchcraft.

as so many people now followed it and old pagan people found it hard to change

2 | 1 | 0

**12.** Describe **in your own words one** effect of the publication of the *Malleus Maleficarum.*

It caused havoc it gave the church the final push to beat non-conformity

2 | 1 | 0

**Look at Paragraph 13.**

**13.** Explain **in your own words** what, according to the writer, was the "beauty of the witch craze".

the brighter the flames the more people were found dead.

2 | 1 | 0

**Look at Paragraph 14.**

**14.** What difference did the 1563 law make to the Church's dealings with "good" and "bad" witches?

even if the witches were 'Good' or 'Bad' they were both killed

2 | 1 | 0

**15.** **Quote** an expression which shows that the distinction between "good" and "bad" is important to modern witches.

"fundemental to an understanding"

2 | ■ | 0

*Marks*

**Look at Paragraphs 15 and 16.**

16. "... the black-hatted old crone as modern stereotype"

Explain **in your own words** what evidence there is that "one aspect of that stereotype is true".

that more of the ~~witches~~ witches

were women

2 | 1 | 0

17. Why were wisewomen often "an easy target"?

as they were always giving info

or wisdom handed down In generations

2 | 1 | 0

**Look at Paragraph 17.**

18. **In your own words**, state what the writer knows about the number of present-day witches.

He believes ~~that there~~ is still some

but many hide

2 | 1 | 0

19. The writer gives two reasons for people's interest in joining witches' covens. **In your own words**, explain each as fully as you can.

(i) they want to return the to

past / be ~~like~~ like the past.

2 | 1 | 0

(ii)

2 | 1 | 0

**Look at Paragraph 18.**

20. **Quote** a word or expression which shows that small birds are no longer sacrificed in Wiccan rituals.

"now defunct"

2 | ■ | 0

*Marks*

**Look at Paragraph 19.**

21. (*a*) What impression does the writer give of the average modern witch?

the are modern, like everyone else.

2 ■ 0

(*b*) Give **two** examples of how the writer conveys this impression.

2 1 0

(i) called Harry or Morag

(ii) live inb the country or counsil house.

**Think about the passage as a whole.**

22. The tone of this article is at times humorous.

(*a*) **Quote one** example of the writer's use of humour.

2 ■ 0

(*b*) Explain fully how the humorous effect is achieved.

2 1 0

23. (*a*) What do you consider the writer's attitude to witches to be?

fair, he dosen't have anything against them.

2 1 0

(*b*) By detailed reference to the content of the article, give a reason for your answer to (*a*).

2 1 0

*[END OF QUESTION PAPER]*

SCOTTISH CERTIFICATE OF EDUCATION 1998

WEDNESDAY, 6 MAY
2.30 PM – 3.20 PM

ENGLISH
STANDARD GRADE
Credit Level
Reading
Text

Read carefully the passage overleaf. It will help if you read it twice. When you have done so, answer the questions. Use the spaces provided in the Question/Answer booklet.

*In this extract the writer gives his impressions of an area of Montana called the Badlands*

1    *Mauvaises terres.* The first missionary explorers had given the place this name, a translation of the Plains Indian term meaning something like hard-to-travel country, for its daunting walls and pinnacles and buttresses of eroded sandstone and sheer clay. Where I was now, in Fallon County, Montana, close to the North Dakota state line, the Badlands were getting better. A horseback rider wouldn't have too much difficulty getting past the blisters and eruptions that scarred the prairie here. But the land was still bad enough to put one in mind of Neil Armstrong and the rest of the Apollo astronauts: dusty, cratered, its green turning to sere yellow under the June sun.

2    Breasting the regular swells of land, on a red dirt road as true as a line of longitude, the car was like a boat at sea. The ocean was hardly more solitary than this empty country, where in forty miles or so I hadn't seen another vehicle. A warm westerly blew over the prairie, making waves, and when I wound down the window I heard it growl in the dry grass like surf. For gulls, there were killdeer plovers, crying out their name as they wheeled and skidded on the wind. *Keel-dee-a, Keel-dee-a.* The surface of the land was as busy as a rough sea—it broke in sandstone outcrops, low buttes, ragged bluffs, hollow combers of bleached clay, and was fissured with waterless creek beds, ash-white, littered with boulders. Brown cows nibbled at their shadows on the open range.

3    The road ahead tapered to infinity, in stages. Hill led to hill led to hill, and at each summit the road abruptly shrank to half its width, then half its width again, until it became a hairline crack in the land, then a faint wobble in the haze, then nothing. From out of the nothing now came a speck. It disappeared. It resurfaced as a smudge, then as a fist-sized cloud. A while passed. Finally, on the nearest of the hilltops, a full-scale dust-storm burst into view. The storm enveloped a low-slung pick-up truck, which slowed and came to a standstill beside the car, open window to open window.

4    "Run out of gas?"

5    "No"—I waved the remains of a hideous sandwich. "Just having lunch."

6    The driver wore a stetson, once white, which in age had taken on the colour, and some of the texture, of a ripe Gorgonzola cheese. Behind his head, a big-calibre rifle was parked in a gun-rack. I asked the man if he was out hunting, for earlier in the morning I'd seen herds of pronghorn antelope; they had bounded away from the car on spindly legs, the white signal-flashes on their rumps telegraphing *Danger!* to the rest. But no, he was on his way into town to go to the store. Around here, men wore guns as part of their everyday uniform, packing Winchesters to match their broad-brimmed hats and high-heeled boots. While the women I had seen were dressed in

nineties clothes, nearly all the men appeared to have stepped off the set of a period Western. Their quaint costume gave even the most arthritic an air of strutting boyishness that must have been a trial to their elderly wives.

7    "Missed a big snake back there by the crick." He didn't look at me as he spoke, but stared fixedly ahead, with the wrinkled long-distance gaze that solo yachtsmen, forever searching for landfall, eventually acquire.

8    "He was a real beauty. I put him at six feet or better. It's a shame I didn't get him—I could have used the rattle off of that fellow . . ."

9    With a blunt-fingered hand the size of a dinner plate, he raked through the usual flotsam of business cards, receipts, spent ball-points and candy wrappings that had collected in the fold between the windshield and the dash. "Some of my roadkills," he said. Half a dozen snake rattles, like whelk shells, lay bunched in his palm.

10    "Looks like you have a nice little hobby there."

11    "It beats getting bit."

12    He seemed in no particular hurry to be on his way, and so I told him where I came from, and he told where he came from. His folks had homesteaded about eight miles over in *that* direction—and he wagged his hat brim southwards across a treeless vista of withered grass, pink shale and tufty sage. They'd lost their place back in the thirties. "The dirty thirties." Now he was on his wife's folks' old place, a dozen miles up the road. He had eleven sections up there.

13    A section is a square mile. "That's quite a chunk of Montana. What do you farm?"

14    "Mostly cattle. We grow hay. And a section and a half is wheat, some years, when we get the moisture for it."

15    "And it pays?"

16    "One year we make quite a profit, and the next year we go twice as deep as that in the hole. That's about the way it goes, round here."

17    "That's the way farmers like to say it goes just about everywhere, isn't it?"

18    We sat on for several minutes in an amiable silence punctuated by the cries of the killdeer and the faulty muffler of the pick-up. Then the man said, "Nice visiting with you," and eased forward. In the rear-view mirror I watched his storm of dust sink behind the brow of a hill.

19    In the nineteenth century, when ships under sail crossed paths in mid-ocean, they "spoke" to each other with signal flags; then, if sea conditions were right, they hove to, lowered boats, and the two captains, each seated in his gig, would have a "gam", exchanging news as they bobbed on the wavetops. In *Moby-Dick*, Melville devoted a chapter to the custom, which was evidently still alive and well on this ocean-like stretch of land. It was so empty that two strangers could feel they had a common bond simply because they were encircled by the same horizon. Here it was a hard and fast rule for drivers to slow down and salute anyone else whom they met on the road, and it was considered a courtesy to stop and say howdy. Fresh from the city, I was dazzled by the antique good manners of the Badlands.

Adapted from *Bad Land* by Jonathan Raban

[*END OF PASSAGE*]

## QUESTIONS

**Write your answers in the spaces provided.**

**Look at Paragraph 1.**

1. (a) Who were the first people to see the Badlands, according to this paragraph?

_____

2 ■ 0

(b) Explain clearly how you know.

_____

_____

2 1 0

2. Explain clearly what made the Badlands "hard-to-travel" before reaching Fallon County.

_____

_____

_____

2 1 0

3. ". . . blisters and eruptions that scarred the prairie . . ."
Explain what this expression adds to the writer's description of the area in Fallon County.

_____

_____

_____

2 1 0

**Look at Paragraph 2.**

4. **Quote** an expression that emphasises the straightness of the road the writer was travelling and explain why it is effective.

_____

_____

_____

2 1 0

Marks

**5.** (*a*) In the first sentence of this paragraph, what is it that makes the car seem "like a boat at sea"?

_____

_____

2 | 1 | 0

(*b*) Show how the writer continues this idea in the rest of the paragraph.

_____

_____

_____

_____

2 | 1 | 0

**Look at Paragraph 3.**

**6.** "The road . . . tapered to infinity . . ."

Explain how the CONTENT and STRUCTURE of the **second sentence** in Paragraph 3 help to make the meaning of this expression clear.

CONTENT   _____

_____

_____

_____

2 | 1 | 0

STRUCTURE _____

_____

_____

_____

2 | 1 | 0

*Marks*

7. Explain how you are made to "see" the approach of the pick-up truck as the writer saw it.

_____

_____

_____

_____    2 | 1 | 0

**Look at Paragraphs 4 to 6.**

8. What **two** things led the writer to ask the driver of the truck if he was hunting?    2 | 1 | 0

   (i) _____

   (ii) _____

9. (*a*) What **three** aspects of the **men's costumes** reminded the writer of "the set of a period Western"?    2 | 1 | 0

   (i) _____

   (ii) _____

   (iii) _____

   (*b*) **In your own words,** explain what **effect** was created by these costumes.

   _____

   _____

   _____    2 | 1 | 0

   (*c*) Why do you think this effect "must have been a trial" to their wives?

   _____

   _____

   _____    2 | 1 | 0

*Marks*

**Look at Paragraphs 7 to 11.**

**10.** What "nice little hobby" did the truck driver appear to have?

_____

_____    2 | 1 | 0


**11.** **Quote two** expressions from this section that continue the comparison between the prairie and the ocean.    2 | 1 | 0

   (i)  _____

   (ii)  _____


**Look at Paragraphs 12 to 17.**

**12.** The truck-driver is a homesteader or farmer.

Why might this area seem an unlikely place for a farm?

_____

_____    2 | 1 | 0


**13.** **In your own words**, explain why the truck driver did **not** grow wheat every year.

_____

_____    2 | ■ | 0


**14.** Explain, **in your own words**, what it is that farmers complain of "just about everywhere".

_____

_____    2 | 1 | 0

Marks

**Look at Paragraphs 18 and 19.**

15. **Quote** an expression that suggests that, despite being strangers, the two men were quite comfortable in each other's company.

_____  2 ■ 0

16. What can you infer about the behaviour of people who live **in the city**? Explain how you arrived at your answer.

_____

_____

_____  2 1 0

17. Explain fully why the writer refers to the novel *Moby-Dick* in the final paragraph.

_____

_____

_____  2 1 0

**Think about the passage as a whole.**

18. Jonathan Raban's main purpose in this piece of writing is to share his experience of the Badlands.

What feature of the writing most helps him to achieve this purpose?

Refer to at least one example of the feature you choose.

_____

_____

_____

_____  2 1 0

*[END OF QUESTION PAPER]*

SCOTTISH
CERTIFICATE OF
EDUCATION
1999

FRIDAY, 30 APRIL
2.30 PM – 3.20 PM

ENGLISH
STANDARD GRADE
Credit Level
Reading
Text

Read carefully the passage. It will help if you read it twice. When you have done so, answer the questions. Use the spaces provided in the Question/Answer booklet.

*Patrick Chamoiseau remembers his childhood on the Caribbean island of Martinique.*

1    Fort-de-France had not yet declared war on the rats. Along with the crabs, they infested the crumbling sidewalks and canals of the city. They haunted the gullies. They scoured the basements; they emerged from the nocturnal refuse. Absorbed with his spiders, his cockroaches and his dragonflies, the little boy didn't notice them right away. A few squeaks here and there. A fleeting shadow in the canal. But during one of his moments of stillness on the roof of the kitchens, he came upon a fabulous spectacle.

2    At about one in the afternoon, Fort-de-France became lethargic, with fewer pedestrians and fewer horns. People sought refuge in the shade to eat. The dust of this urban desert began to flutter. Behind the house, on the roof of the kitchens, a shadow offered a cool haven for the little boy. On Saturday afternoons the languor deepened. Finally, the house creaked under the weight of silence and the little boy was free to do nothing, to be still. It was on a day like this when a squeak lifted him from his inner emptiness, calling him to the edge of the roof. That's when he saw the rats, down in the courtyard. Five or six, yes, there they were—scourers searching for crumbs, tub climbers, tightrope artists on the edge of buckets, disappearing into the kitchens and reappearing just as fast. Very young rats and very old rats. Others, fearful, emerged from the covered canal only to pounce on a titbit of food.

3    Among the rats there was one that was older than the others: slower, more wary, but more powerful and more cunning. He ventured into the open only in conditions of complete security, against a backdrop of pure silence. Not until the floorboards of the house stopped moving, and the town shut down and gave in to the dust, did the old rat risk his shadow beneath the vertical heel of the sun. He was massive, and stitched up with scars; he had lost an ear, a piece of his tail, and perhaps also some part of himself which made him no longer merely a rat. He was so experienced it was terrifying: his heart didn't leap at every puff of wind, but his finely tuned ear and acute eye told him when to disappear instantly. He had no habits, never passed the same spot twice and never retreated in the same manner. This was the rat the boy chose as his very first victim.

4    A strange relationship developed. The boy found a piece of string and created a slip-knot which he laid out in the courtyard. In the middle, he set down a piece of sausage. And with the knot wedged in place, the string in his fist, he sat lookout on the roof.

5    The idea was to lasso the vicious old rat. But the animal must have disliked sausage or else the sight of the lasso cast him into a strategic sadness which kept him in his hole, philosophizing about dark rat affairs. Whatever the case, he never showed up. It was always a younger, stupider rat who ventured into the slip-knot and lunged for the sausage. The boy pulled with all his might—he must have pulled a thousand times. But eventually he had to accept the impossibility of catching a rat with this sausage-lasso set-up. The knot would close around itself, and the impatient boy would haul up nothing but a dangling string.

6    His next contraption was a basin weighted down by a rock. A piece of wood connected to an invisible string held it in the air. The old rat (he never turned up) was supposed to venture underneath in order to collect the bait. Those who did risk it raced off with the sausage as if conscious of the trap. At other, rarer, times they fled empty-mouthed. After a while, not a single one came. There was the flaming gourd, the infernal jar, the superglue, the rubber band, the guillotine-knife, the poison syrup, the terrifying scissor of doom . . . But even this arsenal of small cruelties was not enough to snare the slightest hint of rat. Too late, he learned that he had to suppress his own smell from the traps, and could never reuse a bait. The rats would avoid any dubious windfalls that lay invitingly within tooth's reach. The boy took some time to understand that, in fact, rats were intelligent.

7    One day the old rat spotted him. Standing on the edge of the tub, he furtively glanced his way, then pursued his quest. Two inhuman orbs of opaque blackness served as his eyes. For a split second these eyes brushed over him, and, in a certain sense, scorned him. Never again did the old rat, even though he knew the boy was watching, grant him a second glance. He modified his routes and always remained far from the overhang of the roof where the boy—changing his tactics, trying to be selective—was perched, rock in hand, directly above the bait on the ground, waiting to crush the Old Man's back.

8    Hours of lookout were required, the rock held in his outstretched hand above the void: lying on the tin, watching with only one eye, hoping for silence, breathing in calmness, turning to rust in order to melt into the roof, praying for the old rat to approach, ignoring the other rats that dared to nibble the bait.

9    Towards the end the boy's stiffened arms would drop the vengeful rock on any frenzied latecomers; but even these avoided being crushed, with leaps that became increasingly leisurely. Their losses beneath the far-too-slow moving stone never amounted to more than a snippet of tail, a tuft of hair. Around these measly trophies the boy organized pagan ceremonies.

10    The old rat disappeared sometimes, not to be seen for several weeks.  The little boy supposed him dead.  He imagined secret cemeteries visited by night.  He imagined the streets covered with all these exhausted rats, who knew their way around poison and who, suddenly hearing some obscure call, would set out to dig a grave with their last tooth.  He imagined his ageing adversary, a rat isolated by his years: so much intelligence, such cunning, such caution, so much genius—all ending in dirty dereliction, with no address other than death and forgetting.  So the boy arranged funerals for him on tiny cars.  A box of matches served as a coffin.  The procession travelled the hallway and ended in a liturgy he improvised himself, in rat language.  A burial concluded this ceremony—in a hole gouged in the wall near the stairs.  The boy would go away melancholy, missing his old friend, until one day he would see him reappear.  Then, rather than rejoicing, he would dash off to invent some atrocity capable of finishing him off, this time for real.

11    He watched him grow old.  It was nothing: a stiffness in the back, a misshapen silhouette, the constant shaking of an ear.  He was horrified to see him take risks, react slowly.  He caught the Old Man nibbling things he had scoffed at before; and often he seemed immobile, distracted in a senile kind of way.  The boy watched him fall apart.  A feeling of pity rose up in him: he felt no desire to kill, only the horror of a benign commiseration.  He often had the impression that if he came down from the roof, the Old Man would wait for him and allow himself to be touched.

12    One day, the Old Man limped towards the bait, right under the rock which the boy still brandished, out of habit, from the heights of his lookout.  He advanced with a kind of blind,—or desperate, or absent-minded-faith, something like a suicidal impulse, or the sense that he had little to lose.  He stepped into the trap and began chewing like a cockroach on the bait.

13    The stone did not crush his skull: it had become the keystone of a cathedral of pity in the child, who wept.

Adapted from Carol Volk's translation of *Childhood* by Patrick Chamoiseau

**[END OF PASSAGE]**

## QUESTIONS

### Write your answers in the spaces provided.

**Look at Paragraphs 1 and 2.**

1. (*a*) Explain how the writer, in **Paragraph 1**, emphasises the **number** of rats inhabiting the city of Fort-de-France.

27 "had not yet declared war on the rats" showing that they would need an "army" to get rid of them.

2 | 1 | 0

(*b*) Given that there were so many rats around, explain **in your own words** why the little boy had not noticed them.

✓ Because they were with all the other insects he had

2 | 1 | 0

2. ". . . Fort-de-France became lethargic . . ." (Paragraph 2)

(*a*) What does this mean and why do you think it happened?

2 | 1 | 0

(*b*) **Quote** an expression used later in Paragraph 2 that suggests a similar idea.

the finely tuned and acute eye

2 | ■ | 0

Marks

3. In Paragraph 1, what the boy saw is called a "fabulous spectacle".

Use the information in **Paragraph 2** to answer.

(a) What **exactly** did the little boy see?

Young and old rats

2 1 0

(b) Why does he refer to it as a "a fabulous spectacle"?

because it was wonderful
to see.

2 1 0

**Look at Paragraph 3.**

4. (a) **In your own words, explain** in what ways the old rat was superior to the others.

He was wiser

2 1 0

(b) **Quote** the expression that suggests that the old rat had almost supernatural powers.

His finely tuned ear and acute eye told
him when to dissapear

2 1 0

5. What do you find effective about the **last sentence** of this paragraph? Why?

The way the writer said this was
the boys victim seems really
deadly,

2 1 0

*Marks*

**Look at Paragraphs 4 and 5.**

**6.** (*a*) When using his "sausage-lasso set-up", why did the boy fail to catch,

    (i) the old rat?

      The rat was to clever

    (ii) any of the younger rats?

                                        2 | 1 | 0

    (*b*) **Quote** the expression which suggests that the boy persisted with this method for some time.

    But eventually he had to accept...

                                          2 | ■ | 0

**Look at Paragraphs 6 to 9.**

**7.** What made the boy think that the rats knew the basin "contraption" was a trap?

    They were too intelligent they could smell him.

                                        2 | ■ | 0

**8.** **In your own words**, explain why his "arsenal of small cruelties" failed to "snare the slightest hint of rat".

    because he was there.

                                          2 | 1 | 0

**9.** What conclusion did the boy eventually reach?

    He threw the stone on any rat

                                          2 | ■ | 0

Marks

**10.** "One day the old rat spotted him." (Paragraph 7)

(a) **Quote** the expression that suggests the **lack of concern** in the way the old rat looked at the boy.

he furitevly glanced his way then persued his guest.

2 ■ 0

(b) **In your own words**, what suggests the old rat was, however, nervous of the boy's presence?

he stayed in one place

2 1 0

**11.** ". . . was perched, rock in hand . . ." (Paragraph 7)

What does the writer's use of the word "perched" add to the image created that a simpler word like "sitting" would not?

perched gives the idea he is a bird catching his pray.

2 1 0

**12.** Explain what is unusual about the expression "measly trophies".

trophies are said to be wonderful rewards, he uses the word measley in front to show it isn't that good.

2 1 0

**Look at Paragraph 10.**

**13.** The writer chooses to begin three sentences in a row with the words "He imagined". What does he gain by doing so?

satisfa

2 1 0

Marks

**14.** **In your own words**, what is surprising about the boy's reaction to the old rat's reappearance?

*he was more determined*

*—to do what ?*

2 1 0

**Look at Paragraphs 11, 12 and 13.**

**15.** "The boy watched him fall apart." (Paragraph 11)

**In your own words**, list **three** things that betrayed the fact that the old rat was beginning to fail.

2 1 0

(i) *he limped towards the bait.*

(ii) *nibbling at things he'd eaten before*

(iii) *seemed immobile*

**16.** (*a*) **Quote** the expression from **Paragraph 12** which suggests that the boy did not have much confidence in his latest trap.

2 ■ 0

(*b*) ". . . like a cockroach . . ." (Paragraph 12)

What does this expression suggest about the boy's attitude to the rat's action and why does it do so?

*Scavenger, disgusting*

2 1 0

Marks

**Think about the passage as a whole.**

17. Which **one** of the following words **best** describes the boy's attitude to the old rat throughout the passage? Tick (✓) the appropriate box.

| CONTEMPTUOUS | |
|---|---|
| OBSESSIVE | ✓ |
| FEARFUL | |
| DISMISSIVE | |

Justify your selection, **using evidence from the text**.

He watched him grow old.

2 1 0

18. What do you find effective about the **last paragraph** as an ending to the passage as a whole? Support your answer with **evidence from the text**.

Imagery of death with keystone, cathedral the child cried.

2 1 0

*[END OF QUESTION PAPER]*

SCOTTISH
CERTIFICATE OF
EDUCATION
1999

FRIDAY, 30 APRIL
9.15 AM – 10.30 AM

# ENGLISH
# STANDARD GRADE
Foundation, General
and Credit Levels
Writing

**Read This First**

1   Inside this booklet, there are photographs and words.
Use them to help you when you are thinking about what to write.
Look at all the material and think about all the possibilities.

2   There are 23 assignments altogether for you to choose from.

3   Decide which assignment you are going to attempt.
Choose only **one** and write its number in the margin of your answer book.

4   Pay close attention to what you are asked to write.
**Plan** what you are going to write.
Read and check your work before you hand it in.
Any changes to your work should be made clearly.

FIRST      **Look at the pictures opposite.**

NEXT      Think about growing up.

WHAT YOU HAVE TO WRITE

1. "A voyage of discovery" is another way of describing childhood.

   **Write about your** most important childhood discoveries.

   **OR**

2. **Write about** the ways your experience of growing up has influenced **your** views on bringing up children.

   **OR**

3. Pop stars are good rôle models for young people.

   **Discuss this view.**

   **OR**

4. Think about a time you were separated from a member of your family.

   **Write about** your thoughts and feelings when this happened.

FIRST     **Look at the picture opposite.**

NEXT     Think about appearances
both usual and unusual.

---

## WHAT YOU HAVE TO WRITE

5. "I can't because everyone will look at me."

   **Write about** a time when you had to overcome shyness.
   Concentrate on your **thoughts** and **feelings**.

   **OR**

6. Extreme fashion can cause conflict
   between young people and their parents,
   for example music, clothes and body image.

   **Discuss.**

   **OR**

7. "Individual but all the same."

   **Write about** how **you** cope with pressure from
   friends to go along with their ideas and
   interests.

   **OR**

8. "You're not going out like that!"

   **Write a short story *or* a personal account
   *or* a drama script** suggested by these words.

   **OR**

9. **Write a short story** with the title
   "Behind the Mask".

FIRST      **Look at the pictures opposite.**

NEXT      Think about gambling and its effects.

---

| WHAT YOU HAVE TO WRITE |
|---|

10. **Write an article** for a teenage magazine outlining the dangers gambling can have for young people.

    **OR**

11. **Write a short story** in which the central character gets involved in gambling to try to solve his or her problems.

    **OR**

12. "Spend, spend, spend."

    If **you** were to win a large sum of money how would you make use of it?

    **OR**

13. "A gamble that paid off?"

    **Write about** a time you took a chance . . .